YOUR PERSONAL HOROSCOPE 2019

SCORPIO

GW00712331

Your Personal Horoscope 2019

Scorpio

24th October–22nd November

igloobooks

Published in 2018
by Igloo Books Ltd
Cottage Farm
Sywell
NN6 0BJ
www.igloobooks.com

Copyright © 2018 Foulsham Publishing Ltd

Produced for Igloo Books by Foulsham Publishing Ltd, The Old Barrel Store,
Drayman's Lane, Marlow, Bucks SL7 2FF, England

FIR003 0718
2 4 6 8 10 9 7 5 3 1
ISBN: 978-1-78810-560-6

This is an abridged version of material originally published
in Old Moore's Horoscope and Astral Diary.

Cover designed by Nicholas Gage
Edited by Bobby Newlyn-Jones

Printed and manufactured in China

CONTENTS

1   Introduction   7

2   The Essence of Scorpio
Exploring the Personality of Scorpio the Scorpion   9

3   Scorpio on the Cusp   15

4   Scorpio and its Ascendants   17

5   The Moon and the Part it Plays in your Life   31

6   Moon Signs   35

7   Scorpio in Love   39

8   Venus: The Planet of Love   43

9   Venus through the Zodiac Signs   45

10   Scorpio: 2018 Diary Pages   49

11   Scorpio: 2019 Diary Pages   71

12   Scorpio: 2019 Your Year In Brief   72

13   Rising Signs for Scorpio   157

14   The Zodiac, Planets and Correspondences   159

INTRODUCTION

Your personal horoscopes have been specifically created to allow you to get the most from astrological patterns and the way they have a bearing on not only your zodiac sign, but nuances within it. Using the diary section of the book you can read about the influences and possibilities of each and every day of the year. It will be possible for you to see when you are likely to be cheerful and happy or those times when your nature is in retreat and you will be more circumspect. The diary will help to give you a feel for the specific 'cycles' of astrology and the way they can subtly change your day-to-day life. For example, when you see the sign ☿, this means that the planet Mercury is retrograde at that time. Retrograde means it appears to be running backwards through the zodiac. Such a happening has a significant effect on communication skills, but this is only one small aspect of how the personal horoscope can help you.

With your personal horoscope the story doesn't end with the diary pages. It includes simple ways for you to work out the zodiac sign the Moon occupied at the time of your birth, and what this means for your personality. In addition, if you know the time of day you were born, it is possible to discover your Ascendant, yet another important guide to your personal make-up and potential.

Many readers are interested in relationships and in knowing how well they get on with people of other astrological signs. You might also be interested in the way you appear to very different sorts of individuals. If you are such a person, the section on Venus will be of particular interest. Despite the rapidly changing position of this planet, you can work out your Venus sign, and learn what bearing it will have on your life.

Using your personal horoscope you can travel on one of the most fascinating and rewarding journeys that anyone can take – the journey to a better realisation of self.

THE ESSENCE OF SCORPIO

Exploring the Personality of Scorpio the Scorpion

(24TH OCTOBER – 22ND NOVEMBER)

What's in a sign?

To say that you are a little complicated and somewhat difficult to understand is probably a great understatement. The basic reason for this lies in the peculiar nature of Scorpio rulership. In terms of the elements, your zodiac sign is a Water sign. This makes you naturally emotional, deep, somewhat reserved and ever anxious to help those around you. As a direct contrast, classical astrologers always maintained that your planetary ruler was Mars. Mars is the planet of combat and aggression, being positive and dominant under most circumstances. So it can be judged from the start that there are great contradictions within the basic Scorpio nature.

It's a fact that many people are naturally cautious of Scorpio people. Perhaps this isn't surprising. Under most circumstances you appear to be quiet and peaceful, but the situation is a little like a smoking bomb. When it comes to defending yourself, or in particular those people who you see as being important to you, there is virtually no limit to which you would refuse to go. Generally speaking our ancient ancestors were extremely wise in terms of the names they gave to the different zodiac signs. Consider the apparently diminutive and retiring scorpion. It doesn't go looking for trouble and is generally happy to remain in the shadows. However, if it is provoked, or even attacked, it will take on adversaries many times its own size. It carries a barbed sting in its tail and will strike without any additional warning if necessary.

All the same, the Scorpio reputation may be a little undeserved. Yours is one of the most compassionate and caring of all the zodiac signs. When it comes to working on behalf of humanity, especially the oppressed, the sick or the disenfranchised, you show your true mettle. You cannot stand the thought of people suffering unjustifiably, which is why many of the great social reformers and even freedom fighters had the same zodiac sign as you do.

As a Scorpio you are likely to be intuitive (some would say psychic) and under most circumstances you are more than willing to follow that little voice inside yourself that tells you how to behave in any given situation.

Scorpio resources

Your nature is so very often understated that it might be said that your greatest resource is surprise. You have the ability to shock people constantly, even those who think they understand you perfectly well. This brings us back to the creature for which your zodiac sign is named. A scorpion is diminutive – and would represent a tasty snack for any would-be predator. However, it defies logic by standing its ground and fighting back. When it does, woe betide the aggressor that refuses to take account of its presence. And so it is with you. Quiet, even reserved, you tend to get on with your work. This you do efficiently and without undue fuss, approaching each task with the same methodical attitude. People often don't even realise that you are around. And then, when they least expect it, there you are!

The ability to surprise means that you often get on in life against heavy odds. In addition you have great resilience and fortitude. It is possible for you to continue to work long and hard under circumstances that would force others to retreat. Most Scorpio people would not consider themselves to be tough – in fact quite a few are positively neurotic when it comes to matters associated with their own health. Yet you can endure hardship well and almost always win through in the end.

It's true that you may not be quite as confident as you could be. If you were, people would notice you more and that would detract from that all-important element of surprise that makes you so formidable, and which is definitely the most important weapon in your armoury. However, it is clear that your greatest resource is compassion, and on those occasions when you really allow it to show, you display yourself as being one of the most important allies to your fellow men and women.

At a practical level you are more than capable and can often be expected to perform tasks that you haven't necessarily undertaken before. You have a deep intelligence and good powers to reason things out. Most important of all is a determination that no other zodiac sign can match.

Beneath the surface

This section of an account of the typical Scorpio nature could fill an entire book in itself because you are such a complicated person. However, there are certain advantages to being a Scorpio. For example, nobody is going to run away with the idea that you are basically uncomplicated and shallow. It ought to be clear enough to the dullest observer that there is a boiling, seething volcano bubbling away beneath the surface of almost every Scorpio subject.

You are often accused of having a slightly dark view of life, and it's true that many Scorpio people enjoy a rather morbid curiosity and are fascinated by subjects that make other people shudder. At the same time you could hardly be described as being one of life's natural optimists. Part of the reason for this lies in the fact that you have been disappointed in the past and may have arrived at the conclusion that to expect the worst is often the most sensible course of action. At least that way you are likely to mitigate some of the potential depression regarding failures in the future.

Although this way of thinking is somewhat faulty, it comes so naturally to the Scorpio subject that it actually works very well, though it has to be said that it might be responsible for a tendency to hold back on occasions.

Assessing the way your inner mind works is as difficult for you as it is for any outsider. Even individuals who have been friends for years will sometimes come desperately unstuck if they arrive at the conclusion that they know well what makes you tick. In the recesses of your mind you are passionate, driving, restless, dissatisfied and frequently disappointed with your own efforts. On the other hand, you have the power to make dreams into realities and are excellent at hatching plans that will benefit people far from your own circle and circumstances. Being a tireless worker on behalf of the oppressed, the fate of humanity as a whole is ever an inner concern.

When you love you do so with great width and depth. Your capacity for jealousy knows no bounds and there are times when you can be as destructive to yourself as you ever could be regarding any other individual. Yet for all this your inner mind is lofty and can soar like an eagle on occasions. If the world at large was able to fathom just one tenth of the way your inner mind actually works, people would find you even more fascinating than they do already. But perhaps it's best that they don't. The deepest recesses of Scorpio are an intense secret and will usually stay that way.

11

Making the best of yourself

It isn't hard to find a single word that describes the way you can make the best of yourself, especially when viewed by the world at large. That word is 'communication'. When difficulties arise in your life, especially concerning other people, it's usually because you haven't managed to get your message across, and probably because you haven't even tried to do so. There is much to your nature that is electric, powerful and magnetic. These qualities make you potentially popular and fascinating to a wealth of individuals. Hide these qualities beneath too brusque an exterior and you can seem dark and brooding.

Of course it's a fine line and one that isn't easy to walk. You are constantly worried that if you show people what really makes you tick, they will not find you interesting at all. In reality this concern is totally without foundation. There is more than enough depth about you to last several lifetimes. It doesn't matter how much you give of yourself to the world at large, there are always going to be surprises galore to follow.

Use the dynamic qualities of your nature to the full. Traditionally your ruling planet is Mars – a real go-getter of a planetary ruler and one that imbues you with tremendous power to get things done at a practical level. On the way you need to show how much you care about others. Amidst a plethora of gifts offered to you by the celestial spheres, your ability to help others is likely to be top of the list. When you are giving you are also usually approachable. For you the two go hand in hand. Avoid allowing yourself to become morose or inward looking and always strive to find simple answers to simple questions.

Stick to some sort of work that you find interesting. That can be almost anything to a Scorpio, as long as it feeds the inner you. It does need to carry a degree of diversity and should ideally have an end product that is easy to see. On your journey through life don't get carried away with daydreams – yet on the other hand avoid losing your great potential to make them come true.

The impressions you give

This is one area of your life over which you do have a great deal of control. If the adage 'what you see is what you get' turns out to be true for many signs of the zodiac, it certainly isn't the case with you. The complexity of your nature makes it difficult for even you to find 'the real Scorpio', and in any case this tends to change from day to day. However, regarding some matters there isn't any doubt at all. Firstly you are deeply magnetic and possess the ability to arouse an instinctive fascination in others. Ally this to your propensity for being very positive in your decision making and you have a potentially formidable combination.

Most people already think of you as being an extremely interesting person. Unfortunately they may also occasionally consider you to be a little cool and somewhat difficult to approach. Neither of these impressions are true, it's simply that you are quite shy at heart, and sometimes find it difficult to believe that you could be liked by certain individuals. Learn to throw this erroneous assumption out of the window, and instead, expect to be viewed positively. To do so would make all the difference and would clear the way so that your more personable side can show all the time.

Very few people who know you well could fail to realise that you care deeply, especially about the well-being of the oppressed. You have a truly noble spirit, a fact that shines through in practically everything you do – yet another reason to be noticed.

It's true that you can sometimes make your secretive quality into an art form, which those looking in from the outside might find rather difficult to deal with. This represents another outward aspect of your nature that could so easily be altered. By all means keep your secrets, though not about matters that are of no real note whatsoever. In a single phrase, try to lighten up a little. It's all you need to be almost perfect!

The way forward

It must first be held in mind that Scorpio people are complicated. That's something you simply cannot get away from, no matter how much you might try. On the one hand you can deal with practical matters almost instinctively. You are resourceful, deep thinking, intense and fascinating. On the other side of the coin you are often too fond of luxury and will frequently withdraw yourself from situations that you do not care to pursue. You can be quite stubborn and can even bear a grudge if you feel that you have been provoked.

It is suggested in astrology that no quality of nature is necessarily good or bad, it really depends on the way it is used. For example, stubbornness can be considered a terrible fault, but not if you were being awkward concerning the obvious rights of an oppressed person or group. It turns out that Scorpio has more of a potential to be 'saint or sinner' than any zodiac sign. As long as you examine your motives in any given situation, whilst at the same time trying to cultivate a degree of flexibility that is not one of your natural gifts, then you won't go far wrong.

Turn on the charm when it is necessary because it will rarely if ever let you down. Think about the way you can serve the world, but don't preach about it. Love sincerely, but don't allow jealousy to spoil things. Be constructive in your determination and don't get on your high horse when it isn't necessary. Follow these simple rules for the best chance of progress.

Of course there are many positives around to start with. You are a very loyal friend, are capable of being extremely brave and tend to be very committed to family members. At the same time you are trustworthy and can work long and hard using your own initiative. Although you sometimes worry about your health, you are more robust than most and can endure a high degree of hardship if necessary. You don't take kindly to criticism but can be flexible enough to accept it if you know it is intended for your own good.

Few people doubt your sincerity – that is, when they know what you believe. So it's important to lay your thoughts on the line right from the start. And even if you don't choose to treat the whole world as a friend, you are capable of gathering a little circle around you who would never let you down. Do make sure, however, that this 'inner group' isn't simply comprised of other Scorpios!

SCORPIO ON THE CUSP

Astrological profiles are altered for those people born at either the beginning or the end of a zodiac sign, or, more properly, on the cusps of a sign. In the case of Scorpio this would be on the 24th of October and for two or three days after, and similarly at the end of the sign, probably from the 20th to the 22nd of November.

The Libra Cusp – 24th October to 26th October

You are probably generally considered to be a bright and breezy sort of character, with a great deal of enthusiasm for life. Despite this, few people would doubt that you are a shrewd operator, and that you know what you want and have a fairly good idea of how to go about getting it. Not everyone likes you as much as you would wish, but that's because the Libran side of your nature longs for popularity, while set against this is your deep Scorpio need to speak your mind, even when you know that other people might wish you did not indulge in this trait very frequently.

In love, you typify the split between these two signs. On the one hand you are passionate, sincere and intense, while on the other your Libran responses can cause a certain fickle sort of affection to show sometimes, probably to the confusion of those with whom you are involved at a personal level. Nevertheless, few people would find fault with your basic nature and there isn't much doubt that your heart is in the right place.

When it comes to career matters, you have a very fortunate combination. Scorpio can sometimes be accused of lacking diplomacy, but nothing could be further from the truth with Libra. As a result, you have what it takes in terms of determination but at the same time you are capable of seeing the point of view put forward by colleagues. You tend to rise to the top of the tree and, with your mixture of raw ability and humour that most of the world approves of, you can stay there.

You won't be the sort of person to make quite as many enemies as Scorpio taken alone might do, and you need the cut and thrust of the world much more than the retiring creature after whom your zodiac sign is named. Try not to be controversial and do your best to retain a sense of humour, which is essential to your well-being. Few would doubt the fact that your heart is in the right place and your creative potential could be second to none. Most important of all, you need the self-satisfaction that comes from living in the real world.

The Sagittarius Cusp – 20th November to 22nd November

You can be a really zany character, with a love of life that is second to none. Add to this a penetrating insight, a razor-sharp wit and an instinctive intuition that is quite remarkable and we find in you a formidable person. It's true that not everyone understands what makes you tick, probably least of all yourself, but you strive to be liked and really do want to advertise your willingness to learn and to grow, which isn't always the province of Scorpio when taken alone. Your capacity for work knows no bounds, though you don't really like to get your hands dirty and would feel more content when telling others what to do.

In a career sense, you need to be in a position from which you are able to delegate. This is not because you are afraid of hard work yourself, far from it, but you possess a strong ability to see through problems and you are a natural director of others. Sales careers may interest you, or a position from which you can organise and arrange things. However, you hate to be tied down to one place for long, so you would be at your best when allowed to move around freely and do things in your own way.

You are a natural social reformer, mainly because you are sure that you know what is right and just. In the main you are correct in your assumptions, but there are occasions when you should realise that there is more than one form of truth. Perhaps you are not always quite as patient with certain individuals as you might be but these generally tend to be people who show traits of cruelty or cunning. As a family person, you care very much for the people who figure most prominently in your life. Sometimes you are a definite home bird, with a preference for what you know and love, but this is offset by a restless trend within your nature that often sends you off into the wide blue yonder, chasing rainbows that the Scorpio side of your nature doubts are even there. Few would doubt your charm, your magnetism, or your desire to get ahead in life in almost any way possible. You combine patience with genuine talent and make a loyal, interesting and entertaining friend or lover.

SCORPIO AND ITS ASCENDANTS

The nature of every individual on the planet is composed of the rich variety of zodiac signs and planetary positions that were present at the time of their birth. Your Sun sign, which in your case is Scorpio, is one of the many factors when it comes to assessing the unique person you are. Probably the most important consideration, other than your Sun sign, is to establish the zodiac sign that was rising over the eastern horizon at the time that you were born. This is your Ascending or Rising sign. Most popular astrology fails to take account of the Ascendant, and yet its importance remains with you from the very moment of your birth, through every day of your life. The Ascendant is evident in the way you approach the world, and so, when meeting a person for the first time, it is this astrological influence that you are most likely to notice first. Our Ascending sign essentially represents what we appear to be, while the Sun sign is what we feel inside ourselves.

The Ascendant also has the potential for modifying our overall nature. For example, if you were born at a time of day when Scorpio was passing over the eastern horizon (this would be around the time of dawn) then you would be classed as a double Scorpio. As such, you would typify this zodiac sign, both internally and in your dealings with others. However, if your Ascendant sign turned out to be a Fire sign, such as Aries, there would be a profound alteration of nature, away from the expected qualities of Scorpio.

One of the reasons why popular astrology often ignores the Ascendant is that it has always been rather difficult to establish. We have found a way to make this possible by devising an easy-to-use table, which you will find on page 157 of this book. Using this, you can establish your Ascendant sign at a glance. You will need to know your rough time of birth, then it is simply a case of following the instructions.

For those readers who have no idea of their time of birth it might be worth allowing a good friend, or perhaps your partner, to read through the section that follows this introduction. Someone who deals with you on a regular basis may easily discover your Ascending sign, even though you could have some difficulty establishing it for yourself. A good understanding of this component of your nature is essential if you want to be aware of that 'other person' who is responsible for the way you make contact with the world at large. Your Sun sign, Ascendant sign, and the other pointers in this book will, together, allow you a far better understanding of what makes you tick as an individual. Peeling back the different layers of your astrological make-up can be an enlightening experience, and the Ascendant may represent one of the most important layers of all.

Scorpio with Scorpio Ascendant

This is one of the most potent of all astrological possibilities, but how it is used depends so very much on the individual who possesses it. On the one hand you are magnetic, alluring, sexy, deep and very attractive, whilst at the same time you are capable of being stubborn, self-seeking, vain, over-sensitive and fathomless. It has to be said that under most circumstances the first set of adjectives are the most appropriate, and that is because you keep control of the deeper side, refusing to allow it absolute control over your conscious life. You are able to get almost anything you want from life, but first you have to discover what that might be. The most important factor of all, however, is the way you can offer yourself, totally and without reservation to a needy world.

Self-sacrifice is a marvellous thing, but you can go too far on occasions. The furthest extreme for Scorpios here is a life that is totally dedicated to work and prayer. For the few this is admirable, for the still earth-based, less so. Finding a compromise is not easy as you are not always in touch with yourself. Feed the spiritual, curb the excesses, accept the need for luxury, and be happy.

Scorpio with Sagittarius Ascendant

There are many gains with this combination, and most of you reading this will already be familiar with the majority of them. Sagittarius offers a bright and hopeful approach to life, but may not always have the staying power and the patience to get what it really needs. Scorpio, on the other hand, can be too deep for its own good, is very self-seeking on occasions and extremely giving to others. Both the signs have problems when taken on their own, and, it has to be said, double the difficulties when they come together. But this is not usually the case. Invariably the presence of Scorpio slows down the over-quick responses of the Archer, whilst the inclusion of Sagittarius prevents Scorpio from taking itself too seriously.

Life is so often a game of extremes, when all the great spiritual masters of humanity have indicated that a 'middle way' is the path to choose. You have just the right combination of skills and mental faculties to find that elusive path, and can bring great joy to yourself and others as a result. Most of the time you are happy, optimistic, helpful and a joy to know. You have mental agility, backed up by a stunning intuition, which itself would rarely let you down. Keep a sense of proportion and understand that your depth of intellect is necessary to curb your flighty side.

Scorpio with Capricorn Ascendant

If patience, perseverance and a solid ability to get where you want to go are considered to be the chief components of a happy life, then you should be skipping about every day. Unfortunately this is not always the case and here we have two zodiac signs, both of which can be too deep for their own good. Both Scorpio and Capricorn are inclined to take themselves rather too seriously and your main lesson in life, and some would say the reason you have adopted this zodiac combination, is to 'lighten up'. If all that determination is pushed in the direction of your service to the world at large, you are seen as being one of the kindest people imaginable. This is really the only option for you, because if you turn this tremendous potential power inwards all the time you will become brooding, secretive and sometimes even selfish. Your eyes should be turned towards a needy humanity, which can be served with the dry but definite wit of Capricorn and the true compassion of Scorpio.

It is impossible with this combination to indicate what areas of life suit you the best. Certainly you adore luxury in all its forms, and yet you can get by with almost nothing. You desire travel, and at the same time love the comforts and stability of home. The people who know you best are aware that you are rather special. Listen to what they say.

Scorpio with Aquarius Ascendant

Here we have a combination that shows much promise and a flexibility that allows many changes in direction, allied to a power to succeed, sometimes very much against all the odds. Aquarius lightens the load of the Scorpio mind, turning the depths into potential and making intuitive foresight into a means for getting on in life. There are depths here, because even airy Aquarius isn't too easy to understand, and it is therefore a fact that some people with this combination will always be something of a mystery. However, even this fact can be turned to your advantage because it means that people will always be looking at you. Confidence is so often the key to success in life and the Scorpio–Aquarius mix offers this, or at least appears to do so. Even when this is not entirely the case, the fact that everyone around you believes it to be true is often enough.

You are usually good to know, and show a keen intellect and a deep intelligence, aided by a fascination for life that knows no bounds. When at your best you are giving, understanding, balanced and active. On those occasions when things are not going well for you, beware a stubborn streak and the need to be sensational. Keep it light and happy and you won't go far wrong. Most of you are very, very well loved.

Scorpio with Pisces Ascendant

You stand a chance of disappearing so deep into yourself that other people would need one of those long ladders that cave explorers use, just to find you. It isn't really your fault because both Scorpio and Pisces are Water signs, which are difficult to understand, and you have them both. But that doesn't mean that you should be content to remain in the dark, and the warmth of your nature is all you need to shine a light on the wonderful qualities you possess. But the primary word of warning is that you must put yourself on display and allow others to know what you are, before their appreciation of these facts becomes apparent.

As a server of the world you are second to none and it is hard to find a person with this combination who is not, in some way, looking out for the people around them. Immensely attractive to others, you are also one of the most sought-after lovers. Much of this has to do with your deep and abiding charm, but the air of mystery that surrounds you also helps. Some of you will marry too early, and end up regretting the fact, though the majority of people with Scorpio and Pisces will find the love they deserve in the end. You are able, just, firm but fair, though a sucker for a hard luck story and as kind as the day is long. It's hard to imagine how so many good points could be ignored by others.

Scorpio with Aries Ascendant

The two very different faces of Mars come together in this potent, magnetic and quite awe-inspiring combination. Your natural inclination is towards secrecy, and this fact, together with the natural attractions of the sensual Scorpio nature, makes you the object of great curiosity. This means that you will not go short of attention and should ensure that you are always being analysed by people who may never get to know you at all. At heart you prefer your own company, and yet life appears to find means to push you into the public gaze time and again. Most people with this combination ooze sex appeal and can use this fact as a stepping stone to personal success, yet without losing any integrity or loosening the cords of a deeply moralistic nature.

On those occasions when you do lose your temper, there isn't a character in the length and breadth of the zodiac who would have either the words or the courage to stand against the stream of invective that follows. On really rare occasions you might even scare yourself. A simple look is enough to show family members when you are not amused. Few people are left unmoved by your presence in their life.

Scorpio with Taurus Ascendant

The first, last and most important piece of advice for you is not to take yourself, or anyone else, too seriously. This might be rather a tall order because Scorpio intensifies the deeper qualities of Taurus and can make you rather lacking in the sense of humour that we all need to live our lives in this most imperfect of worlds. You are naturally sensual by nature. This shows itself in a host of ways. In all probability you can spend hours in the bath, love to treat yourself to good food and drink and take your greatest pleasure in neat and orderly surroundings. This can often alienate you from those who live in the same house because other people need to use the bathroom from time to time and they cannot remain tidy indefinitely.

You tend to worry a great deal about things which are really not too important, but don't take this statement too seriously or you will begin to worry about this fact too! You often need to lighten up and should always do your best to tell yourself that most things are not half so important as they seem to be. Be careful over the selection of a life partner and if possible choose someone who is naturally funny and who does not take life anywhere near as seriously as you are inclined to do. At work you are more than capable and in all probability everyone relies heavily on your wise judgements.

Scorpio with Gemini Ascendant

What you are and what you appear to be can be two entirely different things with this combination. Although you appear to be every bit as chatty and even as flighty as Gemini tends to be, nothing could be further from the truth. In reality you have many deep and penetrating insights, all of which are geared towards sorting out potential problems before they come along. Few people would have the ability to pull the wool over your eyes, and you show a much more astute face to the world than is often the case for Gemini taken on its own. The level of your confidence, although not earth-shattering, is much greater with this combination, and you would not be thwarted once you had made up your mind.

There is a slight danger here, however, because Gemini is always inclined to nerve problems of one sort or another. In the main these are slight and fleeting, though the presence of Scorpio can intensify reactions and heighten the possibility of depression, which would not be at all fortunate. The best way round this potential problem is to have a wealth of friends, plenty to do and the sort of variety in your life that suits your Mercury ruler. Financial success is not too difficult to achieve because you can easily earn money and then manage to hold on to it.

Scorpio with Cancer Ascendant

There are few more endearing zodiac combinations than this one. Both signs are Watery in nature and show a desire to work on behalf of humanity as a whole. The world sees you as being genuinely caring, full of sympathy for anyone in trouble and always ready to lend a hand when it is needed. You are a loyal friend, a great supporter of the oppressed and a lover of home and family. In a work sense you are capable, and command respect from your colleagues, even though this comes about courtesy of your quiet competence and not as a result of anything that you might happen to say.

But we should not get too carried away with external factors, or the way that others see you. Inside you are a boiling pool of emotion. You feel more strongly, love more deeply and hurt more fully than any other combination of the Water signs. Even those who think they know you really well would get a shock if they could take a stroll around the deeper recesses of your mind. Although these facts are true, they may be rather beside the point because it is a fact that the truth of your passion, commitment and deep convictions may only surface fully half a dozen times in your life. The fact is that you are a very private person at heart and you don't know how to be any other way.

Scorpio with Leo Ascendant

A Leo with intensity, that's what you are. You are mad about good causes and would argue the hind leg off a donkey in defence of your many ideals. If you are not out there saving the planet you could just be at home in the bath, thinking up the next way to save humanity from its own worst excesses. In your own life, although you love little luxuries, you are sparing and frugal, yet generous as can be to those you take to. It's a fact that you don't like everyone, and of course the same is true in reverse. It might be easier for you to understand why you can dislike than to appreciate the reverse side of the coin, for your pride can be badly dented on occasions. Scorpio brings a tendency to have down spells, though the fact that Leo is also strongly represented in your nature should prevent them from becoming a regular part of your life.

It is important for you to learn how to forgive and forget, and there isn't much point in bearing a grudge because you are basically too noble to do so. If something goes wrong, kiss the situation goodbye and get on with the next interesting adventure, of which there are many in your life. Stop–start situations sometimes get in the way, but there are plenty of people around who would be only too willing to lend a helping hand.

Scorpio with Virgo Ascendant

This is intensity carried through to the absolute. If you have a problem, it is that you fail to externalise all that is going on inside that deep, bubbling cauldron that is your inner self. Realising what you are capable of is not a problem; these only start when you have to make it plain to those around you what you want. Part of the reason for this is that you don't always understand yourself. You love intensely and would do absolutely anything for a person you are fond of, even though you might have to inconvenience yourself a great deal on the way. Relationships can cause you slight problems however, since you need to associate with people who at least come somewhere near to understanding what makes you tick. If you manage to bridge the gap between yourself and the world that constantly knocks on your door, you show yourself to be powerful, magnetic and compulsive.

There are times when you definitely prefer to stay quiet, though you do have a powerful ability to get your message across when you think it is necessary to do so. There are people around who might think that you are a push-over but they could easily get a shock when you sense that the time is right to answer back. You probably have a very orderly house and don't care for clutter of any sort.

Scorpio with Libra Ascendant

There is some tendency for you to be far more deep than the average Libran would appear to be and for this reason it is crucial that you lighten up from time to time. Every person with a Scorpio quality needs to remember that there is a happy and carefree side to all events and your Libran quality should allow you to bear this in mind. Sometimes you try to do too many things at the same time. This is fine if you take the casual overview of Libra, but less sensible when you insist on picking the last bone out of every potential, as is much more the case for Scorpio.

When worries come along, as they sometimes will, be able to listen to what your friends have to say and also realise that they are more than willing to work on your behalf, if only because you are so loyal to them. You do have a quality of self-deception, but this should not get in the way too much if you combine the instinctive actions of Libra with the deep intuition of your Scorpio component.

Probably the most important factor of this combination is your ability to succeed in a financial sense. You make a good manager, but not of the authoritarian sort. Jobs in the media or where you are expected to make up your mind quickly would suit you, because there is always an underpinning of practical sense that rarely lets you down.

THE MOON AND THE PART IT PLAYS IN YOUR LIFE

In astrology the Moon is probably the single most important heavenly body after the Sun. Its unique position, as partner to the Earth on its journey around the solar system, means that the Moon appears to pass through the signs of the zodiac extremely quickly. The zodiac position of the Moon at the time of your birth plays a great part in personal character and is especially significant in the build-up of your emotional nature.

Your Own Moon Sign

Discovering the position of the Moon at the time of birth has always been notoriously difficult because tracking the complex zodiac positions of the Moon is not easy. This process has been reduced to three simple stages with our Lunar Tables. A breakdown of the Moon's zodiac positions can be found from page 35 onwards, so that once you know what your Moon Sign is, you can see what part this plays in the overall build-up of your personal character.

If you follow the instructions on the next page you will soon be able to work out exactly what zodiac sign the Moon occupied on the day that you were born and you can then go on to compare the reading for this position with those of your Sun sign and your Ascendant. It is partly the comparison between these three important positions that goes towards making you the unique individual you are.

How To Discover Your Moon Sign

This is a three-stage process. You may need a pen and a piece of paper but if you follow the instructions below the process should only take a minute or so.

STAGE 1 First of all you need to know the Moon Age at the time of your birth. If you look at Moon Table 1, on page 33, you will find all the years between 1921 and 2019 down the left side. Find the year of your birth and then trace across to the right to the month of your birth. Where the two intersect you will find a number. This is the date of the New Moon in the month that you were born. You now need to count forward the number of days between the New Moon and your own birthday. For example, if the New Moon in the month of your birth was shown as being the 6th and you were born on the 20th, your Moon Age Day would be 14. If the New Moon in the month of your birth came after your birthday, you need to count forward from the New Moon in the previous month. Whatever the result, jot this number down so that you do not forget it.

STAGE 2 Take a look at Moon Table 2 on page 34. Down the left hand column look for the date of your birth. Now trace across to the month of your birth. Where the two meet you will find a letter. Copy this letter down alongside your Moon Age Day.

STAGE 3 Moon Table 3 on page 34 will supply you with the zodiac sign the Moon occupied on the day of your birth. Look for your Moon Age Day down the left hand column and then for the letter you found in Stage 2. Where the two converge you will find a zodiac sign and this is the sign occupied by the Moon on the day that you were born.

Your Zodiac Moon Sign Explained

You will find a profile of all zodiac Moon Signs on pages 35 to 38, showing in yet another way how astrology helps to make you into the individual that you are. In each daily entry of the Astral Diary you can find the zodiac position of the Moon for every day of the year. This also allows you to discover your lunar birthdays. Since the Moon passes through all the signs of the zodiac in about a month, you can expect something like twelve lunar birthdays each year. At these times you are likely to be emotionally steady and able to make the sort of decisions that have real, lasting value.

MOON TABLE 1

YEAR	SEP	OCT	NOV	YEAR	SEP	OCT	NOV	YEAR	SEP	OCT	NOV
1921	2	1/30	29	1954	27	26	25	1987	23	22	21
1922	21	20	19	1955	16	15	14	1988	11	10	9
1923	10	10	8	1956	4	4	2	1989	29	29	28
1924	28	28	26	1957	23	23	21	1990	19	18	17
1925	18	17	16	1958	13	12	11	1991	8	8	6
1926	7	6	5	1959	3	2/31	30	1992	26	25	24
1927	25	25	24	1960	21	20	19	1993	16	15	14
1928	14	14	12	1961	10	9	8	1994	5	5	3
1929	3	2	1	1962	28	28	27	1995	24	24	22
1930	22	20	19	1963	17	17	15	1996	13	11	10
1931	12	11	9	1964	6	5	4	1997	2	2/31	30
1932	30	29	27	1965	25	24	22	1998	20	20	19
1933	19	19	17	1966	14	14	12	1999	9	9	8
1934	9	8	7	1967	4	3	2	2000	27	27	26
1935	27	27	26	1968	23	22	21	2001	17	17	16
1936	15	15	14	1969	11	10	9	2002	6	6	4
1937	4	4	3	1970	1	1/30	29	2003	26	25	24
1938	23	23	22	1971	19	19	18	2004	13	12	11
1939	13	12	11	1972	8	8	6	2005	3	2	1
1940	2	1/30	29	1973	27	26	25	2006	22	21	20
1941	21	20	19	1974	16	15	14	2007	12	11	9
1942	10	10	8	1975	5	5	3	2008	30	29	28
1943	29	29	27	1976	23	23	21	2009	19	18	17
1944	17	17	15	1977	13	12	11	2010	8	8	6
1945	6	6	4	1978	2	2/31	30	2011	27	27	25
1946	25	24	23	1979	21	20	19	2012	6	15	13
1947	14	14	12	1980	10	9	8	2013	4	4	2
1948	3	2	1	1981	28	27	26	2014	23	22	22
1949	23	21	20	1982	17	17	15	2015	13	12	11
1950	12	11	9	1983	7	6	4	2016	1	30	29
1951	1	1/30	29	1984	25	24	22	2017	20	20	18
1952	19	18	17	1985	14	14	12	2018	9	9	7
1953	8	8	6	1986	4	3	2	2019	28	27	26

TABLE 2

DAY	OCT	NOV
1	a	e
2	a	e
3	a	e
4	b	f
5	b	f
6	b	f
7	b	f
8	b	f
9	b	f
10	b	f
11	b	f
12	b	f
13	b	g
14	d	g
15	d	g
16	d	g
17	d	g
18	d	g
19	d	g
20	d	g
21	d	g
22	d	g
23	d	i
24	e	i
25	e	i
26	e	i
27	e	i
28	e	i
29	e	i
30	e	i
31	e	–

MOON TABLE 3

M/D	a	b	d	e	f	g	i
0	LI	LI	LI	SC	SC	SC	SA
1	LI	LI	SC	SC	SC	SA	SA
2	LI	SC	SC	SC	SA	SA	CP
3	SC	SC	SC	SA	SA	CP	CP
4	SC	SA	SA	SA	CP	CP	CP
5	SA	SA	SA	CP	CP	AQ	AQ
6	SA	CP	CP	CP	AQ	AQ	AQ
7	SA	CP	CP	AQ	AQ	PI	PI
8	CP	CP	CP	AQ	PI	PI	PI
9	CP	AQ	AQ	AQ	PI	PI	AR
10	AQ	AQ	AQ	PI	AR	AR	AR
11	AQ	PI	PI	PI	AR	AR	TA
12	PI	PI	PI	AR	TA	TA	TA
13	PI	AR	PI	AR	TA	TA	GE
14	AR	AR	AR	TA	GE	GE	GE
15	AR	AR	AR	TA	TA	TA	GE
16	AR	AR	TA	TA	GE	GE	GE
17	AR	TA	TA	GE	GE	GE	CA
18	TA	TA	GE	GE	GE	CA	CA
19	TA	TA	GE	GE	CA	CA	CA
20	GE	GE	GE	CA	CA	CA	LE
21	GE	GE	CA	CA	CA	LE	LE
22	GE	CA	CA	CA	LE	LE	VI
23	CA	CA	CA	LE	LE	LE	VI
24	CA	CA	LE	LE	LE	VI	VI
25	CA	LE	LE	LE	VI	VI	LI
26	LE	LE	VI	VI	VI	LI	LI
27	LE	VI	VI	VI	LI	LI	SC
28	VI	VI	VI	LI	LI	LI	SC
29	VI	VI	LI	LI	LI	SC	SC

AR = Aries, TA = Taurus, GE = Gemini, CA = Cancer, LE = Leo, VI = Virgo,
LI = Libra, SC = Scorpio, SA = Sagittarius, CP = Capricorn, AQ = Aquarius, PI = Pisces

MOON SIGNS

Moon in Aries

You have a strong imagination, courage, determination and a desire to do things in your own way and forge your own path through life.

Originality is a key attribute; you are seldom stuck for ideas although your mind is changeable and you could take the time to focus on individual tasks. Often quick-tempered, you take orders from few people and live life at a fast pace. Avoid health problems by taking regular time out for rest and relaxation.

Emotionally, it is important that you talk to those you are closest to and work out your true feelings. Once you discover that people are there to help, there is less necessity for you to do everything yourself.

Moon in Taurus

The Moon in Taurus gives you a courteous and friendly manner, which means you are likely to have many friends.

The good things in life mean a lot to you, as Taurus is an Earth sign that delights in experiences which please the senses. Hence you are probably a lover of good food and drink, which may in turn mean you need to keep an eye on the bathroom scales, especially as looking good is also important to you.

Emotionally you are fairly stable and you stick by your own standards. Taureans do not respond well to change. Intuition also plays an important part in your life.

Moon in Gemini

You have a warm-hearted character, sympathetic and eager to help others. At times reserved, you can also be articulate and chatty: this is part of the paradox of Gemini, which always brings duplicity to the nature. You are interested in current affairs, have a good intellect, and are good company and likely to have many friends. Most of your friends have a high opinion of you and would be ready to defend you should the need arise. However, this is usually unnecessary, as you are quite capable of defending yourself in any verbal confrontation.

Travel is important to your inquisitive mind and you find intellectual stimulus in mixing with people from different cultures. You also gain much from reading, writing and the arts but you do need plenty of rest and relaxation in order to avoid fatigue.

Moon in Cancer

The Moon in Cancer at the time of birth is a fortunate position as Cancer is the Moon's natural home. This means that the qualities of compassion and understanding given by the Moon are especially enhanced in your nature, and you are friendly and sociable and cope well with emotional pressures. You cherish home and family life, and happily do the domestic tasks. Your surroundings are important to you and you hate squalor and filth. You are likely to have a love of music and poetry.

Your basic character, although at times changeable like the Moon itself, depends on symmetry. You aim to make your surroundings comfortable and harmonious, for yourself and those close to you.

Moon in Leo

The best qualities of the Moon and Leo come together to make you warm-hearted, fair, ambitious and self-confident. With good organisational abilities, you invariably rise to a position of responsibility in your chosen career. This is fortunate as you don't enjoy being an 'also-ran' and would rather be an important part of a small organisation than a menial in a large one.

You should be lucky in love, and happy, provided you put in the effort to make a comfortable home for yourself and those close to you. It is likely that you will have a love of pleasure, sport, music and literature. Life brings you many rewards, most of them as a direct result of your own efforts, although you may be luckier than average and ready to make the best of any situation.

Moon in Virgo

You are endowed with good mental abilities and a keen receptive memory, but you are never ostentatious or pretentious. Naturally quite reserved, you still have many friends, especially of the opposite sex. Marital relationships must be discussed carefully and worked at so that they remain harmonious, as personal attachments can be a problem if you do not give them your full attention.

Talented and persevering, you possess artistic qualities and are a good homemaker. Earning your honours through genuine merit, you work long and hard towards your objectives but show little pride in your achievements. Many short journeys will be undertaken in your life.

Moon in Libra

With the Moon in Libra you are naturally popular and make friends easily. People like you, probably more than you realise, you bring fun to a party and are a natural diplomat. For all its good points, Libra is not the most stable of astrological signs and, as a result, your emotions can be a little unstable too. Therefore, although the Moon in Libra is said to be good for love and marriage, your Sun sign and Rising sign will have an important effect on your emotional and loving qualities.

You must remember to relate to others in your decision-making. Co-operation is crucial because Libra represents the 'balance' of life that can only be achieved through harmonious relationships. Conformity is not easy for you because Libra, an Air sign, likes its independence.

Moon in Scorpio

Some people might call you pushy. In fact, all you really want to do is to live life to the full and protect yourself and your family from the pressures of life. Take care to avoid giving the impression of being sarcastic or impulsive and use your energies wisely and constructively.

You have great courage and you invariably achieve your goals by force of personality and sheer effort. You are fond of mystery and are good at predicting the outcome of situations and events. Travel experiences can be beneficial to you.

You may experience problems if you do not take time to examine your motives in a relationship, and also if you allow jealousy, always a feature of Scorpio, to cloud your judgement.

Moon in Sagittarius

The Moon in Sagittarius helps to make you a generous individual with humanitarian qualities and a kind heart. Restlessness may be intrinsic as your mind is seldom still. Perhaps because of this, you have a need for change that could lead you to several major moves during your adult life. You are not afraid to stand your ground when you know your judgement is right, you speak directly and have good intuition.

At work you are quick, efficient and versatile and so you make an ideal employee. You need work to be intellectually demanding and do not enjoy tedious routines.

In relationships, you anger quickly if faced with stupidity or deception, though you are just as quick to forgive and forget. Emotionally, there are times when your heart rules your head.

Moon in Capricorn

The Moon in Capricorn makes you popular and likely to come into the public eye in some way. The watery Moon is not entirely comfortable in the Earth sign of Capricorn and this may lead to some difficulties in the early years of life. An initial lack of creative ability and indecision must be overcome before the true qualities of patience and perseverance inherent in Capricorn can show through.

You have good administrative ability and are a capable worker, and if you are careful you can accumulate wealth. But you must be cautious and take professional advice in partnerships, as you are open to deception. You may be interested in social or welfare work, which suit your organisational skills and sympathy for others.

Moon in Aquarius

The Moon in Aquarius makes you an active and agreeable person with a friendly, easy-going nature. Sympathetic to the needs of others, you flourish in a laid-back atmosphere. You are broad-minded, fair and open to suggestion, although sometimes you have an unconventional quality which others can find hard to understand.

You are interested in the strange and curious, and in old articles and places. You enjoy trips to these places and gain much from them. Political, scientific and educational work interests you and you might choose a career in science or technology.

Money-wise, you make gains through innovation and concentration and Lunar Aquarians often tackle more than one job at a time. In love you are kind and honest.

Moon in Pisces

You have a kind, sympathetic nature, somewhat retiring at times, but you always take account of others' feelings and help when you can.

Personal relationships may be problematic, but as life goes on you can learn from your experiences and develop a better understanding of yourself and the world around you.

You have a fondness for travel, appreciate beauty and harmony and hate disorder and strife. You may be fond of literature and would make a good writer or speaker yourself. You have a creative imagination and may come across as an incurable romantic. You have strong intuition, maybe bordering on a mediumistic quality, which sets you apart from the mass. You may not be rich in cash terms, but your personal gifts are worth more than gold.

SCORPIO IN LOVE

Discover how compatible you are with people from the same and other parts of the zodiac. Five stars equals a match made in heaven!

Scorpio meets Scorpio

Scorpio is deep, complex and enigmatic, traits which often lead to misunderstanding with other zodiac signs, so a double Scorpio match can work well because both parties understand one another. They will allow each other periods of silence and reflection but still be willing to help, advise and support when necessary. Their relationship may seem odd to others but that doesn't matter if those involved are happy. All in all, an unusual but contented combination. Star rating: *****

Scorpio meets Sagittarius

Sagittarius needs constant stimulation and loves to be busy from dawn till dusk which may mean that it feels rather frustrated by Scorpio. Scorpions are hard workers, too, but they are also contemplative and need periods of quiet which may mean that they appear dull to Sagittarius. This could lead to a gulf between the two which must be overcome. With time and patience on both sides, this can be a lucrative encounter and good in terms of home and family. A variable alliance. Star rating: ***

Scorpio meets Capricorn

Lack of communication is the governing factor here. Neither of this pair are renowned communicators and both need a partner to draw out their full verbal potential. Consequently, Scorpio may find Capricorn cold and unapproachable while Capricorn could find Scorpio dark and brooding. Both are naturally tidy and would keep a pristine house but great effort and a mutual goal is needed on both sides to overcome the missing spark. A good match on the financial side, but probably not an earth-shattering personal encounter. Star rating: **

Scorpio meets Aquarius

This is a promising and practical combination. Scorpio responds well to Aquarius' exploration of its deep nature and so this shy sign becomes lighter, brighter and more inspirational. Meanwhile, Aquarians are rarely as sure of themselves as they like to appear and are reassured by Scorpio's steady and determined support. Both signs want to be kind to the other which is a basis for a relationship that should be warm most of the time and extremely hot occasionally. Star rating: ****

Scorpio meets Pisces

If ever there were two zodiac signs that have a total rapport, it has to be Scorpio and Pisces. They share very similar needs: they are not gregarious and are happy with a little silence, good music and time to contemplate the finer things in life, and both are attracted to family life. Apart, they can have a tendency to wander in a romantic sense, but this is reduced when they come together. They are deep, firm friends who enjoy each other's company and this must lead to an excellent chance of success. These people are surely made for each other! Star rating: *****

Scorpio meets Aries

There can be great affection here, even if the two signs are so very different. The common link is the planet Mars, which plays a part in both these natures. Although Aries is, outwardly, the most dominant, Scorpio people are among the most powerful to be found anywhere. This quiet determination is respected by Aries. Aries will satisfy the passionate side of Scorpio, particularly with instruction from Scorpio. There are mysteries here which will add spice to life. The few arguments that do occur are likely to be awe-inspiring. Star rating: ****

Scorpio meets Taurus

Scorpio is deep – very deep – which may be a problem, because Taurus doesn't wear its heart on its sleeve either. It might be difficult for this pair to get together, because neither is naturally inclined to make the first move. Taurus stands in awe of the power and intensity of the Scorpio mind, while the Scorpion is interested in the Bull's affable and friendly qualities, so an enduring relationship could be forged if the couple ever get round to talking. Both are lovers of home and family, which will help to cement a relationship. Star rating: **

Scorpio meets Gemini

There could be problems here. Scorpio is one of the deepest and least understood of all the zodiac signs, which at first seems like a challenge to intellectual Gemini, who thinks it can solve anything. But the deeper the Gemini digs, the further down Scorpio goes. Meanwhile, Scorpio may be finding Gemini thoughtless, shallow and even downright annoying. Gemini is often afraid of Scorpio's perception and strength, together with the sting in the Scorpion's tail. Anything is possible, but the outlook for this match is less than promising. Star rating: **

Scorpio meets Cancer

This match is potentially a great success, a fact which is often a mystery to astrologers. Some feel it is due to the compatibility of the Water element, but it could also come from a mixture of similarity and difference in the personalities. Scorpio is partly ruled by Mars, which gives it a deep, passionate, dominant and powerful side. Cancerians generally like and respect this amalgam, and recognise something there that they would like to adopt themselves. On the other side of the coin, Scorpio needs love and emotional security which Cancer offers generously. Star rating: *****

Scorpio meets Leo

Stand back and watch the sparks fly! Scorpio has the deep sensitivity of a Water sign but it is also partially ruled by Fire planet Mars, from which it draws great power, and Leo will find that difficult. Leo loves to take charge and really hates to feel psychologically undermined, which is Scorpio's stock-in-trade. Scorpio may find Leo's ideals a little shallow, which will be upsetting to the Lion. Anything is possible, but this possibility is rather slimmer than most. Star rating: **

Scorpio meets Virgo

There are one or two potential difficulties here, but there is also a meeting point from which to overcome them. Virgo is very caring and protective, a trait which Scorpio understands and even emulates. Scorpio will impress Virgo with its serious side. Both signs are consistent, although also sarcastic. Scorpio may uncover a hidden passion in Virgo which all too often lies deep within its Earth-sign nature. Material success is very likely, with Virgo taking the lion's share of the domestic chores and family responsibilities. Star rating: ***

Scorpio meets Libra

Many astrologers have reservations about this match because, on the surface, the signs are so different. However, this couple may find fulfilment because these differences mean that their respective needs are met. Scorpio needs a partner to lighten the load, which won't daunt Libra, while Libra looks for a steadfast quality which it doesn't possess, but which Scorpio can supply naturally. Financial success is possible because they both have good ideas and back them up with hard work and determination. All in all, a promising outlook. Star rating: ****

VENUS:
THE PLANET OF LOVE

If you look up at the sky around sunset or sunrise you will often see Venus in close attendance to the Sun. It is arguably one of the most beautiful sights of all and there is little wonder that historically it became associated with the goddess of love. But although Venus does play an important part in the way you view love and in the way others see you romantically, this is only one of the spheres of influence that it enjoys in your overall character.

Venus has a part to play in the more cultured side of your life and has much to do with your appreciation of art, literature, music and general creativity. Even the way you look is responsive to the part of the zodiac that Venus occupied at the start of your life, though this fact is also down to your Sun sign and Ascending sign. If, at the time you were born, Venus occupied one of the more gregarious zodiac signs, you will be more likely to wear your heart on your sleeve, as well as to be more attracted to entertainment, social gatherings and good company. If on the other hand Venus occupied a quiet zodiac sign at the time of your birth, you would tend to be more retiring and less willing to shine in public situations.

It's good to know what part the planet Venus plays in your life for it can have a great bearing on the way you appear to the rest of the world and since we all have to mix with others, you can learn to make the very best of what Venus has to offer you.

One of the great complications in the past has always been trying to establish exactly what zodiac position Venus enjoyed when you were born because the planet is notoriously difficult to track. However, we have solved that problem by creating a table that is exclusive to your Sun sign, which you will find on the following page.

Establishing your Venus sign could not be easier. Just look up the year of your birth on the next page and you will see a sign of the zodiac. This was the sign that Venus occupied in the period covered by your sign in that year. If Venus occupied more than one sign during the period, this is indicated by the date on which the sign changed, and the name of the new sign. For instance, if you were born in 1950, Venus was in Libra until the 28th October, after which time it was in Scorpio. If you were born before 28th October your Venus sign is Libra, if you were born on or after 28th October, your Venus sign is Scorpio. Once you have established the position of Venus at the time of your birth, you can then look in the pages which follow to see how this has a bearing on your life as a whole.

1921 LIBRA / 14.11 SCORPIO
1922 SAGITTARIUS / 16.11 SCORPIO
1923 SCORPIO / 9.11 SAGITTARIUS
1924 VIRGO / 3.11 LIBRA
1925 SAGITTARIUS / 7.11 CAPRICORN
1926 LIBRA / 29.10 SCORPIO
1927 VIRGO / 10.11 LIBRA
1928 SAGITTARIUS /
    17.11 CAPRICORN
1929 LIBRA / 13.11 SCORPIO
1930 SAGITTARIUS / 16.11 SCORPIO
1931 SCORPIO / 8.11 SAGITTARIUS
1932 VIRGO / 2.11 LIBRA
1933 SAGITTARIUS / 7.11 CAPRICORN
1934 LIBRA / 29.10 SCORPIO
1935 VIRGO / 10.11 LIBRA
1936 SAGITTARIUS /
    16.11 CAPRICORN
1937 LIBRA / 13.11 SCORPIO
1938 SAGITTARIUS / 16.11 SCORPIO
1939 SCORPIO / 7.11 SAGITTARIUS
1940 VIRGO / 2.11 LIBRA
1941 SAGITTARIUS / 7.11 CAPRICORN
1942 LIBRA / 28.10 SCORPIO
1943 VIRGO / 10.11 LIBRA
1944 SAGITTARIUS /
    16.11 CAPRICORN
1945 LIBRA / 13.11 SCORPIO
1946 SAGITTARIUS / 16.11 SCORPIO
1947 SCORPIO / 6.11 SAGITTARIUS
1948 VIRGO / 1.11 LIBRA
1949 SAGITTARIUS / 6.11 CAPRICORN
1950 LIBRA / 28.10 SCORPIO
1951 VIRGO / 10.11 LIBRA
1952 SAGITTARIUS /
    16.11 CAPRICORN
1953 LIBRA / 12.11 SCORPIO
1954 SAGITTARIUS / 28.10 SCORPIO
1955 SCORPIO / 6.11 SAGITTARIUS
1956 VIRGO / 1.11 LIBRA
1957 SAGITTARIUS / 6.11 CAPRICORN
1958 LIBRA / 27.10 SCORPIO
1959 VIRGO / 10.11 LIBRA
1960 SAGITTARIUS /
    15.11 CAPRICORN
1961 LIBRA / 12.11 SCORPIO
1962 SAGITTARIUS / 28.10 SCORPIO
1963 SCORPIO / 5.11 SAGITTARIUS
1964 VIRGO / 31.10 LIBRA
1965 SAGITTARIUS / 6.11 CAPRICORN
1966 LIBRA / 27.10 SCORPIO
1967 VIRGO / 10.11 LIBRA
1968 SAGITTARIUS /
    15.11 CAPRICORN
1969 LIBRA / 11.11 SCORPIO
1970 SAGITTARIUS / 28.10 SCORPIO

1971 SCORPIO / 4.11 SAGITTARIUS
1972 VIRGO / 31.10 LIBRA
1973 SAGITTARIUS / 6.11 CAPRICORN
1974 LIBRA / 26.10 SCORPIO
1975 VIRGO / 9.11 LIBRA
1976 SAGITTARIUS /
    15.11 CAPRICORN
1977 LIBRA / 11.11 SCORPIO
1978 SAGITTARIUS / 28.10 SCORPIO
1979 SCORPIO / 4.11 SAGITTARIUS
1980 VIRGO / 30.10 LIBRA
1981 SAGITTARIUS / 5.11 CAPRICORN
1982 LIBRA / 26.10 SCORPIO
1983 VIRGO / 9.11 LIBRA
1984 SAGITTARIUS /
    14.11 CAPRICORN
1985 LIBRA / 10.11 SCORPIO
1986 SAGITTARIUS / 28.10 SCORPIO
1987 SCORPIO / 3.11 SAGITTARIUS
1988 VIRGO / 30.10 LIBRA
1989 SAGITTARIUS / 5.11 CAPRICORN
1990 LIBRA / 25.10 SCORPIO
1991 VIRGO / 9.11 LIBRA
1992 SAGITTARIUS /
    14.11 CAPRICORN
1993 LIBRA / 10.11 SCORPIO
1994 SAGITTARIUS / 28.10 SCORPIO
1995 SCORPIO / 3.11 SAGITTARIUS
1996 VIRGO / 29.10 LIBRA
1997 SAGITTARIUS / 5.11 CAPRICORN
1998 LIBRA / 25.10 SCORPIO
1999 VIRGO / 9.11 LIBRA
2000 SAGITTARIUS /
    14.11 CAPRICORN
2001 LIBRA / 10.11 SCORPIO
2002 SAGITTARIUS / 28.10 SCORPIO
2003 SCORPIO / 3.11 SAGITTARIUS
2004 VIRGO / 29.10 LIBRA
2005 SAGITTARIUS / 5.11 CAPRICORN
2006 LIBRA / 25.10 SCORPIO
2007 VIRGO / 9.11 LIBRA
2008 SAGITTARIUS /
    14.11 CAPRICORN
2009 LIBRA / 10.11 SCORPIO
2010 SAGITTARIUS / 28.10 SCORPIO
2011 SCORPIO / 3.11 SAGITTARIUS
2012 VIRGO / 29.10 LIBRA
2013 SAGITTARIUS / 5.11 CAPRICORN
2014 LIBRA / 25.10 SCORPIO
2015 VIRGO / 9.11 LIBRA
2016 SAGITTARIUS /
    13.11 CAPRICORN
2017 LIBRA / 10.11 SCORPIO
2018 SAGITTARIUS / 28.10 SCORPIO
2019 SCORPIO/ 03.11 SAGITTARIUS

VENUS THROUGH THE ZODIAC SIGNS

Venus in Aries

Amongst other things, the position of Venus in Aries indicates a fondness for travel, music and all creative pursuits. Your nature tends to be affectionate and you would try not to create confusion or difficulty for others if it could be avoided. Many people with this planetary position have a great love of the theatre, and mental stimulation is of the greatest importance. Early romantic attachments are common with Venus in Aries, so it is very important to establish a genuine sense of romantic continuity. Early marriage is not recommended, especially if it is based on sympathy. You may give your heart a little too readily on occasions.

Venus in Taurus

You are capable of very deep feelings and your emotions tend to last for a very long time. This makes you a trusting partner and lover, whose constancy is second to none. In life you are precise and careful and always try to do things the right way. Although this means an ordered life, which you are comfortable with, it can also lead you to be rather too fussy for your own good. Despite your pleasant nature, you are very fixed in your opinions and quite able to speak your mind. Others are attracted to you and historical astrologers always quoted this position of Venus as being very fortunate in terms of marriage. However, if you find yourself involved in a failed relationship, it could take you a long time to trust again.

Venus in Gemini

As with all associations related to Gemini, you tend to be quite versatile, anxious for change and intelligent in your dealings with the world at large. You may gain money from more than one source but you are equally good at spending it. There is an inference here that you are a good communicator, via either the written or the spoken word, and you love to be in the company of interesting people. Always on the look-out for culture, you may also be very fond of music, and love to indulge the curious and cultured side of your nature. In romance you tend to have more than one relationship and could find yourself associated with someone who has previously been a friend or even a distant relative.

Venus in Cancer

You often stay close to home because you are very fond of family and enjoy many of your most treasured moments when you are with those you love. Being naturally sympathetic, you will always do anything you can to support those around you, even people you hardly know at all. This charitable side of your nature is your most noticeable trait and is one of the reasons why others are naturally so fond of you. Being receptive and in some cases even psychic, you can see through to the soul of most of those with whom you come into contact. You may not commence too many romantic attachments but when you do give your heart, it tends to be unconditionally.

Venus in Leo

It must become quickly obvious to almost anyone you meet that you are kind, sympathetic and yet determined enough to stand up for anyone or anything that is truly important to you. Bright and sunny, you warm the world with your natural enthusiasm and would rarely do anything to hurt those around you, or at least not intentionally. In romance you are ardent and sincere, though some may find your style just a little overpowering. Gains come through your contacts with other people and this could be especially true with regard to romance, for love and money often come hand in hand for those who were born with Venus in Leo. People claim to understand you, though you are more complex than you seem.

Venus in Virgo

Your nature could well be fairly quiet no matter what your Sun sign might be, though this fact often manifests itself as an inner peace and would not prevent you from being basically sociable. Some delays and even the odd disappointment in love cannot be ruled out with this planetary position, though it's a fact that you will usually find the happiness you look for in the end. Catapulting yourself into romantic entanglements that you know to be rather ill-advised is not sensible, and it would be better to wait before you committed yourself exclusively to any one person. It is the essence of your nature to serve the world at large and through doing so it is possible that you will attract money at some stage in your life.

Venus in Libra

Venus is very comfortable in Libra and bestows upon those people who have this planetary position a particular sort of kindness that is easy to recognise. This is a very good position for all sorts of friendships and also for romantic attachments that usually bring much joy into your life. Few individuals with Venus in Libra would avoid marriage and since you are capable of great depths of love, it is likely that you will find a contented personal life. You like to mix with people of integrity and intelligence but don't take kindly to scruffy surroundings or work that means getting your hands too dirty. Careful speculation, good business dealings and money through marriage all seem fairly likely.

Venus in Scorpio

You are quite open and tend to spend money quite freely, even on those occasions when you don't have very much. Although your intentions are always good, there are times when you get yourself in to the odd scrape and this can be particularly true when it comes to romance, which you may come to late or from a rather unexpected direction. Certainly you have the power to be happy and to make others contented on the way, but you find the odd stumbling block on your journey through life and it could seem that you have to work harder than those around you. As a result of this, you gain a much deeper understanding of the true value of personal happiness than many people ever do, and are likely to achieve true contentment in the end.

Venus in Sagittarius

You are lighthearted, cheerful and always able to see the funny side of any situation. These facts enhance your popularity, which is especially high with members of the opposite sex. You should never have to look too far to find romantic interest in your life, though it is just possible that you might be too willing to commit yourself before you are certain that the person in question is right for you. Part of the problem here extends to other areas of life too. The fact is that you like variety in everything and so can tire of situations that fail to offer it. All the same, if you choose wisely and learn to understand your restless side, then great happiness can be yours.

Venus in Capricorn

The most notable trait that comes from Venus in this position is that it makes you trustworthy and able to take on all sorts of responsibilities in life. People are instinctively fond of you and love you all the more because you are always ready to help those who are in any form of need. Social and business popularity can be yours and there is a magnetic quality to your nature that is particularly attractive in a romantic sense. Anyone who wants a partner for a lover, a spouse and a good friend too would almost certainly look in your direction. Constancy is the hallmark of your nature and unfaithfulness would go right against the grain. You might sometimes be a little too trusting.

Venus in Aquarius

This location of Venus offers a fondness for travel and a desire to try out something new at every possible opportunity. You are extremely easy to get along with and tend to have many friends from varied backgrounds, classes and inclinations. You like to live a distinct sort of life and gain a great deal from moving about, both in a career sense and with regard to your home. It is not out of the question that you could form a romantic attachment to someone who comes from far away or be attracted to a person of a distinctly artistic and original nature. What you cannot stand is jealousy, for you have friends of both sexes and would want to keep things that way.

Venus in Pisces

The first thing people tend to notice about you is your wonderful, warm smile. Being very charitable by nature you will do anything to help others, even if you don't know them well. Much of your life may be spent sorting out situations for other people, but it is very important to feel that you are living for yourself too. In the main, you remain cheerful, and tend to be quite attractive to members of the opposite sex. Where romantic attachments are concerned, you could be drawn to people who are significantly older or younger than yourself or to someone with a unique career or point of view. It might be best for you to avoid marrying whilst you are still very young.

SCORPIO:
2018 DIARY PAGES

October 2018

1 MONDAY
Moon Age Day 22   Moon Sign Gemini

You remain dynamic and enthusiastic. Not only do you have all the vitality and power you could require, you also have masses of charm and a winning personality that nobody could ignore. This really is a major-league time for you and should be treated as one of the best phases of the year in an all-round sense.

2 TUESDAY
Moon Age Day 23   Moon Sign Cancer

Your partner could be quite difficult to please for the next couple of days and what might make matters worse is that the Sun is still in your solar twelfth house. This means you are slightly lacking in tact and won't have quite the level of confidence in your own abilities and opinions that is often the case.

3 WEDNESDAY
Moon Age Day 24   Moon Sign Cancer

Partnerships are now favourably highlighted and co-operation becomes the unequivocal key to success. Out here in the middle of the week you should be quite satisfied with your efforts and you seem to have what it takes to be especially popular when you are in good company. Get on with jobs you find interesting and stimulating.

4 THURSDAY
Moon Age Day 25   Moon Sign Leo

Get down to brass tacks today as far as money is concerned and order your finances in a very positive sort of way. This is also a time during which you can afford to indulge yourself more than you normally would and you should also find that your friends are anxious to show you their generosity.

5 FRIDAY
Moon Age Day 26   Moon Sign Leo

You work best when you are involved in an interesting social environment and as a result you might not be trying too hard to get much done in a practical sense today. Your judgement is sound and you are able to get onside with the sort of people who rarely fail to get things done. You may even decide to follow their lead later.

6 SATURDAY
Moon Age Day 27   Moon Sign Virgo

You are probably your own worst critic today, which is something of a shame at a time when things ought to be going very well for you. If you do lack patience with yourself you will not do as well as you would if you remained optimistic regarding the outcome of any situation. Keep abreast of local news and views at this time.

7 SUNDAY
Moon Age Day 28   Moon Sign Virgo

Romantically and personally you are likely to be on a winning streak and the intensity of positive situations is now likely to be so great you would be quite unlikely to miss out on any of the benefits coming in your direction. Stand up for friends in disputes but wherever possible talk your way out of awkward situations.

8 MONDAY
Moon Age Day 29   Moon Sign Virgo

Home and family are vital issues for you at the best of times but they seem to be more important than ever as the Moon moves on in your chart later today. You will most likely be entering a new phase in terms of a personal attachment and younger family members will now be more likely to turn to you for practical help and advice.

9 TUESDAY
Moon Age Day 0   Moon Sign Libra

Today you are more inclined to see things in terms of the way they will have a bearing on your personal and family life. The world beyond your own door is not quite as important as might sometimes be the case and you become a slightly more private sort of person. This is not at all unusual for Scorpio from time to time.

10 WEDNESDAY *Moon Age Day 1   Moon Sign Libra*

The focus is on finance and it looks as though you will already be finding ways to improve things, even if the plans you put into action today won't mature for a week or two. At the same time you now tend to be slightly more outgoing and there are likely to be invitations around that will draw you out of your own little corner.

11 THURSDAY *Moon Age Day 2   Moon Sign Scorpio*

Today you are calling the shots and the lunar high brings the best possible potential for a time of fun and happy encounters. Don't be too keen to keep busy all the time because you are very socially inclined at present and will want to please yourself. Break out while you can and get well away from the usual concerns of a routine Thursday.

12 FRIDAY *Moon Age Day 3   Moon Sign Scorpio*

You should be feeling very energetic and you won't be at all tardy when it comes to getting involved in anything that stretches your abilities and offers excitement. Your financial standing should be slightly improved – or else you begin to discover that you can raise money in previously unknown ways.

13 SATURDAY *Moon Age Day 4   Moon Sign Sagittarius*

Don't rely entirely on your intuition when it comes to important matters. As a rule your almost psychic nature is your best guide but this probably isn't the case now. It is facts and figures that really count, together with the tried-and-tested advice of people who have done the same thing you are facing now time and again.

14 SUNDAY *Moon Age Day 5   Moon Sign Sagittarius*

A significant boost to teamwork and group activities comes along today, courtesy of the rapidly moving Moon. In any situation it is important not to let your own perceived limitations hold you back but rather to have confidence in your ability to learn as you go along. Experience is a fine thing but it has to come from doing a job.

15 MONDAY   *Moon Age Day 6   Moon Sign Capricorn*

There could be some pressure upon you now to rethink your strategies regarding work-based issues but it might be best to stick to your own guns with things as they are in a planetary sense. Of course you need to show yourself willing to listen to another point of view but in the end it is your opinions that really count.

16 TUESDAY   *Moon Age Day 7   Moon Sign Capricorn*

There could be a few practical mishaps today and you might be too inclined to rush things. Try to settle to what you are doing and make sure you do things one at a time. There ought to be a great deal of attention coming to you from people who are especially fond of you and practical help is in place if you need it.

17 WEDNESDAY   *Moon Age Day 8   Moon Sign Capricorn*

When it comes to your social life you will be enjoying a happy and eventful period around now. Any sort of dialogue between yourself and others can provide you with new ideas and a renewed sense of purpose regarding practical issues. You will also be doing what you can to create comfortable surroundings at home.

18 THURSDAY   *Moon Age Day 9   Moon Sign Aquarius*

You might be forced to change your mind about something major today. There are some unusual situations coming to light and all sorts of odd coincidences could crowd in on your day. Don't let them spook you and merely treat them as signposts towards a better future – if you take note of them.

19 FRIDAY   *Moon Age Day 10   Moon Sign Aquarius*

As the days go on you will discover that your ego is growing stronger and that you develop better and better ways to make people take notice of you. This process begins now as several planets edge themselves onward in your solar chart. People might not be hanging on your every word but they are at least looking your way.

20 SATURDAY *Moon Age Day 11   Moon Sign Pisces*

Keep well organised and it looks as though you won't go far wrong. Although there is no particular rush about life just at the moment you will recognise that it would be best to grab opportunities whilst they are around. Friends will be equally busy and might not always be able to drop everything just to suit your particular needs.

21 SUNDAY *Moon Age Day 12   Moon Sign Pisces*

It's time to be broadening your personal horizons. It's a fact about autumn-born Scorpio that when many people are starting to slow down for the winter, you are just getting into gear. The thought of shorter days and colder weather does little or nothing to dent your enthusiasm and you should be especially optimistic today.

22 MONDAY *Moon Age Day 13   Moon Sign Pisces*

Keep your eyes open because there are new opportunities about, all of which seem custom-made to bring more fun into your life. You are now much more resilient and are determined to break down barriers if necessary in order to get where you want to be. Romance is especially well starred at present.

23 TUESDAY *Moon Age Day 14   Moon Sign Aries*

What you really manage to do at the moment is to get the very best out of almost everyone you come across. Part of this is down to astrological influences but it can be aided by your own attitude, which is now positive and determined. Get in touch with someone who lives at a distance and arrange to visit them.

24 WEDNESDAY *Moon Age Day 15   Moon Sign Aries*

Get out there and make new friends. It is very important at the moment to make the best of impression on just about anyone and this is going to be especially important at work. Mixing business with pleasure isn't something you do all as a rule but it can stand you in good stead under present planetary trends.

25 THURSDAY
Moon Age Day 16   Moon Sign Taurus

This brief period of inactivity is simply a slight pause on the otherwise presently smooth road that is your life. Let the traffic flow on for a while as you stand and watch contentedly. Frustration will only follow if you insist on try to do too much at a time when the prevailing planetary influences are telling you to preserve your energy.

26 FRIDAY
Moon Age Day 17   Moon Sign Taurus

Although it might not seem to be the case as the day gets started most of your efforts around now have success written all over them. A break from everyday routines is still recommended but not so that you can continue to watch and wait. On the contrary you now need to be doing different and stimulating things, alongside your friends.

27 SATURDAY
Moon Age Day 18   Moon Sign Gemini

The Sun is now in your solar first house and brings with it that part of the year during which you can be expected to make significant gains and to be at your best in most situations. You ought to be feeling far more confident than you were a couple of weeks ago and part of this has to do with your ability to work through sticky patches.

28 SUNDAY
Moon Age Day 19   Moon Sign Gemini

You might sense that in some ways a more frugal approach is necessary and if so you will be reining in your spending. It is possible that this attitude has something to do with dawning realisation that Christmas is not far away, or it may simply be that you have a project in mind that will require money.

29 MONDAY
Moon Age Day 20   Moon Sign Cancer

You look and feel strong, which is why almost everyone takes it for granted that you could achieve almost anything. There is no point in telling them that this is not the case, so you may as well believe it yourself. Don't get tied down today with pointless routines but take gains where you find them and push for what you really want.

30 TUESDAY   *Moon Age Day 21   Moon Sign Cancer*

Give and take is important at home, especially if certain family members are behaving in a less that typical way. Fortunately this is not likely to be the case in a romantic sense. In this area of your life you know exactly what to say and will also have a good idea about what makes your partner tick. A timely gift can make all the difference.

31 WEDNESDAY   *Moon Age Day 22   Moon Sign Cancer*

Remove yourself from confrontational situations because you really don't need any arguments in your life just now. You want to be friends with everyone, something that might prove to be difficult but certainly not impossible. They say it takes two to tango and if you don't want to fall out with anyone, nothing will persuade you to do so.

♏ *November* 2018

1 THURSDAY
Moon Age Day 23   Moon Sign Leo

You can now expect to be taking a hands-on role when it comes to creating your own future. Scorpio sometimes feels itself locked up in the needs and opinions of other people but this is far less likely to be the case during the first half of November. A new month means new perspectives, and the necessary energy to get things moving.

2 FRIDAY
Moon Age Day 24   Moon Sign Leo

More than ever today you seem to be taken up with practical ideas and with getting things done as efficiently as you can. You might have to put one or two personal plans on hold because you can't do everything at the same time, no matter how much you try. Pace yourself and try to get as much fun as possible from the day.

3 SATURDAY
Moon Age Day 25   Moon Sign Virgo

You should find that you now have greater control over your life and its circumstances. This is part of the legacy of the first house Sun you are enjoying at the moment and you probably find yourself in the midst of an eventful and generally exciting period. Whilst others are gearing down for winter you are as lively as a cricket.

4 SUNDAY
Moon Age Day 26   Moon Sign Virgo

Your powers are generally good and you keep your wits about you under most circumstances now. You can be of tremendous help to your friends and even to people you barely know at all. That's because your powers of discrimination are good and you are quite happy to pass on your acquired wisdom to others.

5 MONDAY
Moon Age Day 27   Moon Sign Libra

The influence you have over certain people is now less certain than it appeared to be a day or two ago. Before you start anything new, especially if it means relying on others, do make sure that the co-operation you need is going to be forthcoming. Slight embarrassment could be the result of taking people for granted today.

6 TUESDAY
Moon Age Day 28   Moon Sign Libra

It would be best not to expect too much from others at this time. When it comes to getting things done you might decide to go it alone and some relationships could be fraught with complications. In the main, life is still going your way and despite minor frustrations you will win through in most important situations.

7 WEDNESDAY
Moon Age Day 0   Moon Sign Scorpio

Now you can break through barriers that may have stood before you for months or even years. Having done so you move into new pastures altogether and can achieve some of the successes that might have eluded you for a while. Seek out someone you haven't seen for ages and renew your contact with them.

8 THURSDAY
Moon Age Day 1   Moon Sign Scorpio

Communication remains the important component of your life, not just because of the lunar high but also on account of the position of the Sun. If you remain quiet today nobody will know what you want and since they find you so charming at the moment getting their assistance to further your own plans is simply a matter of asking.

9 FRIDAY
Moon Age Day 2   Moon Sign Sagittarius

You have a good mind for business and the decisions you make at this time tend to be shot through with perception and wisdom. Avoid confrontations at work by finding ways to agree with others while at the same time managing to get your own way. A little psychology can go a long way right now and this is something you are good at.

10 SATURDAY   *Moon Age Day 3   Moon Sign Sagittarius*

It you are at work you can expect steady and smooth progress, matched by a fairly uneventful but generally peaceful time at home. This may not be the most exciting period of the year but it is solid and dependable. If there is one thing Scorpio respects it is the ability to know what is coming and you also like others to be as reliable as you are.

11 SUNDAY   *Moon Age Day 4   Moon Sign Sagittarius*

The focus is now much more likely to be on your public persona. You won't be hiding your natural abilities but neither will you be brash or outspoken. The combination of charisma, charm and practical common sense that you display now and during the coming week should assure you of great popularity.

12 MONDAY   *Moon Age Day 5   Moon Sign Capricorn*

In the middle of a phase of enhanced social activity there ought to be plenty of opportunities for light relief and for a relaxation where more serious matters are concerned. In many situations you should be able to find the answers you need quickly and are unlikely to be spending endless hours mulling things over.

13 TUESDAY   *Moon Age Day 6   Moon Sign Capricorn*

This may be the best time of all to confide your feelings to loved ones and to get on with sorting things out as far as your home is concerned. Be as sympathetic as you can to those who are presently having difficulties and show just how helpful the sign of Scorpio can be. Avoid pointless routines today because they would bore you.

14 WEDNESDAY   *Moon Age Day 7   Moon Sign Aquarius*

Practical affairs should be looking up. Now is a good time for consolidation as you find the time you need to let others know the way your mind is working on many different levels. Simply sitting around and talking can be very important and you can catch up on all sorts of news you didn't know before.

15 THURSDAY   *Moon Age Day 8   Moon Sign Aquarius*

Look out for a few harsh words today, possibly between yourself and your life partner. If this does happen, find out what is causing the irritation and that means taking time out from a busy schedule to ask a few questions. Any misunderstandings can then be dealt with in no time at all.

16 FRIDAY   *Moon Age Day 9   Moon Sign Aquarius*

Don't get too carried away today because although life looks exciting you also need to focus on what is really important. There are too many distractions around at present and these could cause you to miss something that could bring in money and opportunities later. All that's needed is for you to keep your eyes and ears open.

17 SATURDAY ☿   *Moon Age Day 10   Moon Sign Pisces*

It is clear that you still want to have fun and that you will also be keen to involve as many people as you can in some of your ingenious schemes. Not all of these are going to work out quite the way you might have intended but even if you only succeed in ten percent you will end November somewhat better off than you began it.

18 SUNDAY ☿   *Moon Age Day 11   Moon Sign Pisces*

You really need to feel useful today and will be doing all you can to be supportive of both colleagues and friends. Once the routine aspects of the day are dealt with the time will be right to have some fun. Involve family members if you can but it's especially important to include your partner.

19 MONDAY ☿   *Moon Age Day 12   Moon Sign Aries*

The time seems right to tighten up certain securities – which ought to make you feel more comfortable with your life generally. Not everyone will have your best interests at heart right now but you are shrewd and attentive, which means the chances of anyone duping you are as near to zero as makes no odds.

20 TUESDAY ☿ *Moon Age Day 13   Moon Sign Aries*

There isn't much doubt about your ability to get on extremely well with those people you care about the most but what might be even more important is your response to virtual strangers. The usual Scorpio suspicion seems to be taking a holiday and you make new friends at every turn. One or two of these could prove to be significant.

21 WEDNESDAY ☿ *Moon Age Day 14   Moon Sign Taurus*

The lunar low is underpinned this month by topsy-turvy influences, some of which come like a bolt from the blue and knock your reasoning sideways. Try a few alternative points of view and examine situations carefully before you take any sort of prohibitive action. If it were possible to stand still altogether you should do it.

22 THURSDAY ☿ *Moon Age Day 15   Moon Sign Taurus*

The go-getting side of your personality remains strong, even if you find it somewhat difficult to go and get precisely what you want for today at least. By tomorrow everything should be more or less back to normal, except for the fact that the Sun is moving out of your solar first house and into the somewhat more solid second.

23 FRIDAY ☿ *Moon Age Day 16   Moon Sign Taurus*

Today you should be striving for a peaceful and contented home-life. While this is yours for the taking it is unlikely to be the end of the story because as soon as you sit down in your favourite chair you will become restless and will want to be on the move again. Relatives will marvel at your restlessness.

24 SATURDAY ☿ *Moon Age Day 17   Moon Sign Gemini*

You have what it takes to show yourself in a new light, particularly to people who haven't noticed you at all so far this year. Your energy levels are likely to be high and you revel in any opportunity to get involved with social events. Although you will be extremely busy you still seem to find sufficient time to do almost every you wish.

25 SUNDAY ☿ *Moon Age Day 18   Moon Sign Gemini*

If you want to make sure that everything you say is clearly understood you might have to make your position extremely clear. Don't worry that others will tire of hearing your voice. On the contrary you are going to be just about as popular as it is possible to be, whilst at the same time getting most of what you want from life.

26 MONDAY ☿ *Moon Age Day 19   Moon Sign Cancer*

If business or practical issues are up for discussion you are likely to be taking a leading role. You seem to have some really good ideas at the moment and will be quite happy to throw these in for what they are worth. Don't expect to make too much progress in matters of love today – through no fault of your own.

27 TUESDAY ☿ *Moon Age Day 20   Moon Sign Cancer*

With plenty of enjoyment in mind you are now slightly less likely to be thinking about progress of any sort. The one exception is possibly a desire to do well in sporting activities. Scorpio hates to be beaten and this facet of your nature is probably stronger now than would normally be the case.

28 WEDNESDAY ☿ *Moon Age Day 21   Moon Sign Leo*

What you hear from others today can contribute to the progressive phase you are presently enjoying. The only slight fly in the ointment comes from colleagues or friends who promise more than they deliver. Keep on top of situations and when you see you can't rely on others, get cracking yourself. Your energy levels remain high.

29 THURSDAY ☿ *Moon Age Day 22   Moon Sign Leo*

You simply want to achieve too much and as a result you might find certain projects grinding to a halt. Drop half of your expectations for the moment and concentrate on issues that are very nearly sorted. That way you will also have time to have fun, which is probably more important than anything at the end of November.

30 FRIDAY ☿ *Moon Age Day 23   Moon Sign Virgo*

Almost everything is working well for you as this most fortunate month draws to a close. The realisation that December is about to start could come as something of a shock, if only because you have been too busy to look at the calendar. Spend some time today listening carefully to the opinions of the people with whom you live.

♏

December 2018

1 SATURDAY ☿ *Moon Age Day 24   Moon Sign Virgo*

This would be an ideal time to look again at your money and to decide how best you can use your resources more wisely. Be inventive when it comes to buying your Christmas gifts and don't squander cash on non-essentials. Under the present position of the Sun you should be filled with useful and quite innovative ideas.

2 SUNDAY ☿ *Moon Age Day 25   Moon Sign Libra*

Everything seems to focus on your love life now, and a little extra effort could prove to be quite useful. Make sure the most important person in your life knows how significant they are to you – which means telling them, of course. This is not a good period for taking those you care about for granted.

3 MONDAY ☿ *Moon Age Day 26   Moon Sign Libra*

Property and financial interests are now positively highlighted in your solar chart. You remain basically innovative and filled with good ideas as to how you can increase your fortune and your influence in the days ahead. If you splash out on anything around now it could well be a gift for your partner.

4 TUESDAY ☿ *Moon Age Day 27   Moon Sign Scorpio*

You should be at the very forefront of anything that is happening around you – mostly because you are the one doing all the organising. People will be happy to follow your lead and the lunar high offers you great power over life generally. Make the most of it and go for something you have wanted to do for a long time.

5 WEDNESDAY ☿ *Moon Age Day 28 Moon Sign Scorpio*

Your personality dominates the scene today and you may be inclined to push your ideas forward, even when it is quite obvious that some people do not agree with you. If things begin to go wrong at any stage the last thing you should do is to panic. Simply regroup and start again, slowly and steadily.

6 THURSDAY ☿ *Moon Age Day 29 Moon Sign Scorpio*

The quickened pace of life keeps you on your toes and you begin to enjoy diverse interests to a greater extent. You won't simply be looking in one direction for the answers you need but in many. People generally should seem to be quite helpful and your increased ability to co-operate is part of the reason they are so approachable.

7 FRIDAY *Moon Age Day 0 Moon Sign Sagittarius*

This is a time to be sorting out basic issues ahead of the Christmas period and for deciding what your plans are going to be. Try not to overcrowd your schedule or else instead of benefiting from the upcoming holiday period you risk ending up fatigued. Jettison a few redundant ideas and try to move forward in your thinking.

8 SATURDAY *Moon Age Day 1 Moon Sign Sagittarius*

Your independent mental approach and the way you solve problems makes you popular to have around and is the reason why so many people are likely to be turning to you for advice throughout most of today and in the near future. Part of the reason is that you are thinking on your feet and you ooze confidence.

9 SUNDAY *Moon Age Day 2 Moon Sign Capricorn*

Whilst you might consider that your tendency to speak out and to tell the truth is a positive thing, it is likely that others will not. There are times when a little sugar on the pill is to be recommended and you won't get far today if those closest to you see your attitude as being somewhat brutal. Tact is important so don't forget to use it.

10 MONDAY *Moon Age Day 3   Moon Sign Capricorn*

It is likely that you will be very communicative today and that you will be on the ball when it comes to making little changes at work that can make all the difference in the long-term. Not everyone will be on your side, either professionally or socially but when the chips are down there are many you can rely on.

11 TUESDAY *Moon Age Day 4   Moon Sign Aquarius*

You have so many ideas at the moment it is going to be difficult to get the majority of them off the ground before Christmas period. Certain issues will have to be kept on hold until next year and although this can be frustrating on one level, on another it makes you more excited about the potential for the future.

12 WEDNESDAY *Moon Age Day 5   Moon Sign Aquarius*

There seems to be a great deal of ego and assertiveness around at the moment and at least some of it is coming from your direction. You could be looking towards a period of very hard work and it won't help if you cause problems with the people who can best help you. A little humility now goes a long way.

13 THURSDAY *Moon Age Day 6   Moon Sign Aquarius*

With present trends around you might have to be slightly more frugal than you had been expecting. Perhaps you haven't got everything you need for Christmas yet, whilst at the same time money is short. With a little careful planning you can do what is necessary in terms of gifts whilst spending little and also having fun.

14 FRIDAY *Moon Age Day 7   Moon Sign Pisces*

You crave physical comforts now and will be enlisting the support of loved ones in order to make sure this is possible. Luxury appeals to you, and you won't want to be putting yourself out any more than is strictly necessary. Because you are so loveable it is likely that you receive all the attention you desire.

15 SATURDAY
Moon Age Day 8   Moon Sign Pisces

You are very generous at the moment and that's a good thing, not least of all because you get back much more than you give in one way or another. This would be a good time to enter competitions and to test your skill against others. Social trends are particularly interesting and remain so for some time.

16 SUNDAY
Moon Age Day 9   Moon Sign Pisces

With the accent now firmly on enjoyable communication, you are really looking forward to what Christmas has to offer. For many of you the festive season starts right now and you will be getting into the right frame of mind. Keep an eye on a family member who might have been out of sorts recently.

17 MONDAY
Moon Age Day 10   Moon Sign Aries

You seem to have lots of ideas at your disposal. Even if eight out of ten of them are not workable, that still leaves two that are worth pursuing. With only a few days left until Christmas actually starts, your mind tends to travel back to previous times. There may be a few lessons to be learned from the past.

18 TUESDAY
Moon Age Day 11   Moon Sign Aries

A friendly word in the right ear might make it easy for you to settle a personal issue that has been on your mind. At the same time you can be of significant assistance to colleagues, friends and even your partner. Scorpio is presently at its most co-operative, which enhances your natural popularity.

19 WEDNESDAY
Moon Age Day 12   Moon Sign Taurus

Look out for a little tension that is brought about by the arrival of the lunar low. Such is the speed of your life at the moment that you may almost fail to notice the restrictions that the Moon in Taurus is going to place upon you, though by tomorrow you may be more inclined to feel the brakes being applied.

20 THURSDAY   *Moon Age Day 13   Moon Sign Taurus*

Your fortunes are likely to be in the doldrums but it is unlikely that any major problem is going to emerge. On the contrary you remain generally resilient, even if you have to undertake the same job more than once. Keep your money in your purse or wallet for today and try not to spend more than you have to until a little later.

21 FRIDAY   *Moon Age Day 14   Moon Sign Gemini*

This will most likely be a fairly uneventful and easy-going sort of day and leaves you with plenty of time to lay down those last-minute plans for all that lies ahead of you in the next week or two. Don't allow anyone to push you into any sort of scheme that you don't approve of or about which you have suspicions.

22 SATURDAY   *Moon Age Day 15   Moon Sign Gemini*

Family gatherings ought to be of real interest now and you will be doing more than most to make these possible. Even if you do not come from a very close family background you are likely to feel more attached than usual. A sense of place and belonging is extremely important to you at present.

23 SUNDAY   *Moon Age Day 16   Moon Sign Cancer*

This is a good time during which to try your hand at money making and innovative enterprises. Help with these is certain if you ask around and people generally seem to want to assist you today. There is a quieter side to your nature that shows later but in the main you are happy to be in the social mainstream.

24 MONDAY   *Moon Age Day 17   Moon Sign Cancer*

The arrival of Christmas Eve may bring you much closer to something you have wanted for ages. This should also be a good day for expressing your emotions and for getting onside with your partner. New personalities are likely to enter your life under the social influences of today and you could even make a new friend for life.

25 TUESDAY
Moon Age Day 18   Moon Sign Leo

If Christmas Day fails to bring you your heart's desire it won't be far away. There are a multitude of good planetary aspects surrounding you at the present time and these should conspire to offer you a good time. You need to be in the company of people you love in order to make the most of what is on offer.

26 WEDNESDAY
Moon Age Day 19   Moon Sign Leo

Change and diversity is important for Boxing Day and although you may have stuck around the homestead yesterday you are far less likely to do so today. Your powers of persuasion are at a peak so if there is someone you now want to influence, you could hardly pick a better time than this to turn on the charm and to convince them.

27 THURSDAY
Moon Age Day 20   Moon Sign Virgo

You may now get an opportunity to improve your mind in some way, as well as to learn that you are smarter than you might have thought. You love to pit your wits against those of interesting people, whilst at the same time showing the distinctly competitive edge to your Scorpio nature.

28 FRIDAY
Moon Age Day 21   Moon Sign Virgo

As the holidays progress, look out for a few limitations today as far as your own mind is concerned because you seem to be entering a short phase of relative uncertainty. Gains come today as a result of the generosity of those around you, particularly that of family members.

29 SATURDAY
Moon Age Day 22   Moon Sign Libra

Daily life might be subject to sudden changes and that could mean having to think on your feet a good deal today. Although you will be comfortable at home, it's possible you will be taking some time out to visit relatives and the change of scenery could work to your advantage.

30 SUNDAY
Moon Age Day 23   Moon Sign Libra

This is a great time for communicating well with others. Few people will be at work at the moment but those who are can forge a special bond with colleagues. Ignore the winter weather because it's clear that you need some fresh air in your lungs. Those of you who are away for Christmas probably benefit the most.

31 MONDAY
Moon Age Day 24   Moon Sign Libra

There is no doubt that you are on great form today. You could gain new insight into a subject that is currently uppermost in your mind. Not everyone seems to be on the same wavelength as you but by the end of the day you have plenty of energy and can really enjoy what New Year gatherings have to offer.

SCORPIO:
2019 DIARY PAGES

SCORPIO:
YOUR YEAR IN BRIEF

The accent is definitely on success for Scorpio this year, even if there are a few small distractions along the way. Starting very positively, January and February get the year off to a great start, especially at work. The winter weather won't stop you from being progressive, keen to travel and happy to do whatever is necessary to get ahead. People from the past may return to your life again, bringing with them a few memories.

As the year advances, you will want to be standing up for your rights. March and April should see you willing to go the extra mile to prove a point, but you will need to take care not to create problems for yourself later. It's fine to be proved right but always better to be diplomatic. Friends should be warm and helpful and you might also benefit from the good luck of a relative.

May and June could offer you more in the way of material gains and bring you closer to achieving some longed-for objectives. You will be acting on impulse for much of the time and although this might occasionally lead to trouble, in the main it works well for you. It's time to spoil yourself in some way and if that means spending a few pounds on something you know to be an indulgence, so be it.

July and August see the Sun racing on through the zodiac and reflecting well on you. You are likely to be more passionate at this time and relationships should look good as a result. Take every possible opportunity for travel. People are relying heavily on you during August but you will be a rock at this time and won't let anyone down. You should also be surrounded by some interesting personalities.

With September and October may come one or two minor setbacks but you can use them to hone your already excellent skills at thinking on your feet. People will naturally turn to you for guidance, even in extenuating circumstances. Look out for some excitement, probably brought about as a result of relationships, and make the best of all opportunities to have fun. Money should be easier to come by in October.

The end of the year is likely to bring its own particular challenges, but they are not going to be ones you would shy away from. You may have something to prove during November and December and you will be quite happy to be put to the test, even if others are watching. Scorpio often wants to prove that it's in the right, but around Christmas you may find that co-operation is better than conflict. New starts will certainly coincide with the arrival of a new year.

January 2019

1 TUESDAY
Moon Age Day 25   Moon Sign Scorpio

Even though it's New Year's Day, your ambitions are boosted by the presence of the lunar high. If you decide on a particular course of action, you will stick to it and see it through to the end. Although some jobs could bore you a little, you should undertake them with a good will and plenty of humour.

2 WEDNESDAY
Moon Age Day 26   Moon Sign Scorpio

Don't be afraid to take a little risk, especially when you know in your heart of hearts that you are doing the right thing. There might be all sorts of other people around who behave as though they know better than you do how you should live your life. Whilst the lunar high is around you will be more willing to let them know how you really feel.

3 THURSDAY
Moon Age Day 27   Moon Sign Sagittarius

You should utilise your skill in diplomacy in your dealings with others today. Although you may lack confidence initially, as time wears on you should grow more comfortable. People will be listening to you with great attention and they may take as much from your silences as from your words.

4 FRIDAY
Moon Age Day 28   Moon Sign Sagittarius

Financial matters may be complex at this time. Keep a careful eye on how much you are spending. A few luxuries will be welcome, of course, but not too many. Trends indicate that you should read the small print of any important document carefully, or better still leave signing it until later.

5 SATURDAY
Moon Age Day 0   Moon Sign Capricorn

You may benefit from the input of others when you are looking for new ideas. Listen to people who are coming fresh into your life at this time. Don't be held back by those who speak their minds too freely. You can contribute to your own success by heeding your own common sense.

6 SUNDAY
Moon Age Day 1   Moon Sign Capricorn

Domestic issues may crowd in on you, just at the point in time when you feel the need of some relaxation. Leave anything worrisome on the back burner if you can force yourself to do so. There are people around who will help you out, but can you really be bothered to seek them out just now?

7 MONDAY
Moon Age Day 2   Moon Sign Capricorn

Mental and cultural pursuits can all be uplifting today. It's time to stretch your mind, and there should be no shortage of people willing to join in. You would do well in any sort of quiz now or when put to the test at work. Your powers of recall are good and you will relish any challenge.

8 TUESDAY
Moon Age Day 3   Moon Sign Aquarius

There may be the odd difficulty to overcome today, perhaps because you can't agree with everyone. In normal circumstances, you would brush off anyone who appeared determined to be awkward but trends indicate that you may find this harder today.

9 WEDNESDAY
Moon Age Day 4   Moon Sign Aquarius

Events at work point to satisfying results. Not only should you receive a lot of support from your colleagues, but you should also find that circumstances seem to be bending to your will. You may well feel that fate is on your side in a number of different ways.

10 THURSDAY
Moon Age Day 5   Moon Sign Pisces

Though your powers of persuasion are good at present, there are some people who will not come round to your point of view, no matter what you say to them. Accept this and don't spend too much time trying to move mountains. There are other people to meet and alternative ways to spend your time.

11 FRIDAY
Moon Age Day 6   Moon Sign Pisces

Relationships can prove to be successful for you in a number of ways today. Firstly, you should find that romantic attachments are stronger and more enduring. When it comes to everyday friendships, there may be people around at the moment who are willing to show just how much you mean to them.

12 SATURDAY
Moon Age Day 7   Moon Sign Pisces

Though trends suggest this is a good day to assert yourself professionally, you may not be able to if you do not work on a Saturday. Trends suggest that personal relationships may suffer because others fail to behave in the way you might expect. Ride out this trend by keeping things light-hearted.

13 SUNDAY
Moon Age Day 8   Moon Sign Aries

Today's influences continue to indicate that steady, professional progress can be maintained if you are at work. If your personal life is still under strain, try to focus on other matters. There may be some real personalities around at present and a few of them might materialise in your life now.

14 MONDAY
Moon Age Day 9   Moon Sign Aries

Today, you may need to get an emotional issue out of the way before you are in a position to please yourself and do what takes your fancy. If you are Scorpio who is looking for work, you really should be keeping your eyes open now. Money matters should now be more settled than they were earlier this month.

15 TUESDAY
Moon Age Day 10   Moon Sign Taurus

You need encouragement today, especially from your partner. Unfortunately, this may not be forthcoming and so you will have to soldier on alone for a good deal of the day. This is not a state of affairs that is likely to last long, so don't set too much store by what is, after all, a very temporary phenomenon.

16 WEDNESDAY
Moon Age Day 11   Moon Sign Taurus

You may have to dig deep in order to get to the root cause of an emotional problem today, perhaps not for yourself but on behalf of someone else. Trends clearly indicate that you could be singled out to lend a listening ear – a state of affairs that might not prove to be all that comfortable.

17 THURSDAY
Moon Age Day 12   Moon Sign Taurus

Family responsibilities may have to take second place in your thinking now, as the practical necessities of life get underway following an extended quiet period. Many Scorpios will now be straining at the leash and just aching to get things moving. Patience is still your best quality, however.

18 FRIDAY
Moon Age Day 13   Moon Sign Gemini

Now you are more likely than ever to find yourself in the social limelight, possibly not the most appealing position for you but one you can relish nevertheless. There may be some new arrangements to consider, particularly at home if relatives suddenly decide they don't like things the way they are.

19 SATURDAY
Moon Age Day 14   Moon Sign Gemini

Your winning ways can bring a distinctly romantic streak into your life around this time. You have plenty of energy and a fixed determination regarding the way you want things to be. Others pick up on this, particularly those very close to you in a personal sense.

20 SUNDAY
Moon Age Day 15   Moon Sign Cancer

Expand your horizons at every possible opportunity and make the most of what might be turning into a really excellent weekend. Your innate common sense will underpin the practical qualities that are so much a part of your personality. Rules and regulations are made to be bent or broken today.

21 MONDAY
Moon Age Day 16   Moon Sign Cancer

Prepare for today to be a busy time at work and one during which you have little or no time to cast your mind homeward. This can be rather unnerving for your zodiac sign because a part of you never leaves the comfort and security of your abode. Remain as positive as possible for now.

22 TUESDAY
Moon Age Day 17   Moon Sign Leo

Don't be afraid to take advantage of your natural popularity at the moment. Those around you seem eminently reasonable and quite willing to take your ideas on board. Get as much done as early in the day as you can, leaving yourself with some personal time later on.

23 WEDNESDAY
Moon Age Day 18   Moon Sign Leo

You may succeed particularly well in partnerships in the middle of this working week and might find that you are getting on especially well with people who meant little to you in the past. If you are able to modify your own nature, all sorts of new avenues could now be opened to you.

24 THURSDAY
Moon Age Day 19   Moon Sign Virgo

You want to be the first at work today, such is your competitive edge and the fund of ideas that is flowing through you. Be careful, though, there is just a chance you will exhaust yourself and that won't really be much help in the longer-term. Slow and steady always wins the race for your zodiac sign.

25 FRIDAY   *Moon Age Day 20   Moon Sign Virgo*

Today could prove to be a period of some instability, which is likely to mean that you react to situations rather than create them. Although this can be quite uncomfortable, you are probably going to be better off because of it. Originality is what this period is all about and if it comes from elsewhere, who cares?

26 SATURDAY   *Moon Age Day 21   Moon Sign Libra*

Good times are on the way in regard to your social life, even if you are having slightly more difficulty with regard to work. Best of all is romance because it is in this sphere of your life that you achieve the greatest degree of happiness right now. In business matters you could prove rather too blunt for your own good.

27 SUNDAY   *Moon Age Day 22   Moon Sign Libra*

Personal encounters may be particularly surprising at this time but given that this looks likely to be a very peculiar day all round, perhaps not the most startling! The unusual may become commonplace and you will need to use every bit of your intuition in order to work out what is happening.

28 MONDAY   *Moon Age Day 23   Moon Sign Scorpio*

Meeting people, travelling, reading and writing are all favoured under present trends. The more you learn about life, the greater is your fascination with it. This is likely to be a very varied sort of day and one during which you are fully committed to integrating with the world of which you are a part.

29 TUESDAY   *Moon Age Day 24   Moon Sign Scorpio*

Scorpios are well known to be extremely intense at times, and that quality may become obvious for many of you today. There is a fine line between doing what suits you and upsetting other people, however. It won't be easy to be entirely truthful at present, but you owe it to the ones you care about to at least try.

30 WEDNESDAY *Moon Age Day 25   Moon Sign Sagittarius*

At best you can be very innovative today and that appeals to people who are looking at old tasks in apparently new ways. In discussions you prove that you can mix tact and truthfulness, which is not a skill possessed by all zodiac signs. Relatives may be in need of your attentive ear and unique attitude now.

31 THURSDAY *Moon Age Day 26   Moon Sign Sagittarius*

Colleagues and even your partner could be surprised at your mental resilience and your level of determination. That doesn't mean they fall out with you in any way. On the contrary, all the help and support you need and desire is likely to be with you at the moment. Advantages are easy to come by.

♏ February
2019

1 FRIDAY
Moon Age Day 27   Moon Sign Sagittarius

Professional tasks are likely to keep you rather busy right now and there may not be quite as much time as you would wish for having fun. However, by the evening you may have some hours to please yourself, which you might choose to spend in the company of family members, rather than friends.

2 SATURDAY
Moon Age Day 28   Moon Sign Capricorn

Your desire to get together with others this weekend is strong and as such you might be inclined to put aside some of the usual considerations in order to socialise. You could enjoy an outing of some sort, or take on some practical tasks, just as long as there is someone else around with whom you can have a good chat.

3 SUNDAY
Moon Age Day 29   Moon Sign Capricorn

It is time for a rest, whether you realise it or not. It doesn't really matter how much you choose to push yourself today, it simply won't work. You might just as well sit back and watch life go by. Taking time out to sit and contemplate is very worthwhile today, and will enable you to take stock of what lies ahead.

4 MONDAY
Moon Age Day 0   Moon Sign Aquarius

Once again, you need to take life steadily and to allow others to do some of the running around. If family members especially are not keen to let you have a break, remind them of all you do on their behalf. You engender a good deal of love in others, so they should be willing to spoil you now.

5 TUESDAY   *Moon Age Day 1   Moon Sign Aquarius*

Trends move on and you can keep up with a varied and interesting social life today, which is probably just as well since professional progress appears to be rather limited. If you feel that not everyone is your friend right now, accept this with good grace and don't allow it to push you into unwanted action.

6 WEDNESDAY   *Moon Age Day 2   Moon Sign Aquarius*

Never attempt to force your ideas on to relatives or friends. By all means use a degree of persuasion, but in the end allow people to do things in their own way. The chances are that when you turn on the charm, you are likely to get your own way in any case. All it takes is a little tact.

7 THURSDAY   *Moon Age Day 3   Moon Sign Pisces*

Certain personal issues keep you fully occupied today, so it may be difficult to find the time to do the necessary practical things in life. This being the case, it would be sensible to relinquish some of the control to others. Delegation is the name of the game, both at work and later at home.

8 FRIDAY   *Moon Age Day 4   Moon Sign Pisces*

This is a time to show off your practical skills and prove to anyone who doubts you that you know what you are doing. Try hard at work because promotion could be on the cards and you won't want to pass up any opportunity. For Scorpios who are simply determined to relax today, there could be some luxury in store.

9 SATURDAY   *Moon Age Day 5   Moon Sign Aries*

A lengthy discussion could help you to sort out problems that have been around for a while. Your powers of communication appear to be excellent at the moment, so why not make use of them? Romance is a possibility for many Scorpions at this time, even if you were not expecting it.

10 SUNDAY   *Moon Age Day 6   Moon Sign Aries*

There are lots of interesting ideas in the air. All you need to do is quantify them and work out how best to maximise their potential. If you get the chance of a break from routine and maybe even a journey today, you should grab it with both hands. Don't leave a friend out in the cold with a problem you can easily solve.

11 MONDAY   *Moon Age Day 7   Moon Sign Aries*

Trends bring you the ability to get right to the very heart of practical matters and you should be able to do that one important thing in a situation that can make all the difference in the end. Confidence is what it takes to make this Monday special. You can pretend you have it even if you feel it is lacking. You will be surprise at how convincing you can be.

12 TUESDAY   *Moon Age Day 8   Moon Sign Taurus*

Make sure you are not deceiving yourself when it comes to personal and even intimate decisions at present. It is possible that you need another point of view and there are people around who can deliver on this. A little embarrassment is nothing if you feel very much better in the end.

13 WEDNESDAY   *Moon Age Day 9   Moon Sign Taurus*

This could prove to be a rather routine day, but it might be none the worse for that. It means that you can get through a great many jobs and still feel fresh enough later to find ways and means of enjoying yourself. What you can do right now is to relax while you work, an enviable state of affairs.

14 THURSDAY   *Moon Age Day 10   Moon Sign Gemini*

Today ought to be favourable for progress of a very specific sort. This is not a time when you will be trying to do a thousand different jobs at once, but if your mind is focused, almost anything becomes possible. Not everything will turn out exactly as you would wish but there are occasions when life knows best.

15 FRIDAY
Moon Age Day 11   Moon Sign Gemini

Life is on a roll now and this Friday could prove to be especially interesting. It is true that you may have to persuade someone to do something they are not looking forward to, but this is a minor detail bearing in mind your present amazing ability to talk others round to your particular point of view.

16 SATURDAY
Moon Age Day 12   Moon Sign Cancer

The question arises today as to whether you want to continue in a direction you have previously chosen or change your mind. There is nothing at all wrong with modifying your opinions, even if you have to explain your reasons to someone else. Trends also indicate the possibility of some small financial gains around at this time.

17 SUNDAY
Moon Age Day 13   Moon Sign Cancer

Fulfil your need for variety and stimulation in just about any way you can today. If you work on a Sunday and can take the day off then so much the better. You are good company and great to be around generally. If there are any frustrations at all today, these will come from the direction of people who simply won't adapt.

18 MONDAY
Moon Age Day 14   Moon Sign Leo

You are still involved in a period of change, some of which you haven't chosen yourself. Having to constantly adapt isn't necessarily easy for your zodiac sign but it is very important. If you can manage to shrug your shoulders and simply watch what is happening around you, so much the better.

19 TUESDAY
Moon Age Day 15   Moon Sign Leo

Apart from good trends in personal finances, this may also be a rewarding time for renewing aspects of your personal life. You won't be making too many mistakes, either at work or at home and you should find yourself surrounded by people who quite obviously like you.

20 WEDNESDAY   *Moon Age Day 16   Moon Sign Virgo*

Your talent for understanding others has rarely been better than it is at the moment. This would therefore be a good time to sort out the problems of a friend or even a family member. If, however, you are the one seeking advice, you should turn to a wise old friend.

21 THURSDAY   *Moon Age Day 17   Moon Sign Virgo*

The desire for freedom is strong within you now, though this doesn't necessarily mean you intend to fly off to some exotic location. The sort of freedom you seek has much more to do with being able to go about your life in the way you would wish. If others stand on those rights, it's time to tell them.

22 FRIDAY   *Moon Age Day 18   Moon Sign Libra*

In the practical world, you should now see a general improvement in your finances, though this is not something that will happen overnight. Make the right decisions now and before very long you will be pleased with the way cash is flowing for you. Avoid family arguments because they cannot achieve anything at this time.

23 SATURDAY   *Moon Age Day 19   Moon Sign Libra*

Any form of philosophical interest appeals to you now, especially if it is allied to physical exercise. This is the reason that so many Scorpios enjoy activities such as yoga or tai chi. Workouts for their own sake are not so interesting and so a search for the right path might be beginning.

24 SUNDAY   *Moon Age Day 20   Moon Sign Scorpio*

Now the Moon is firmly settled in your zodiac sign and the time comes for having fun. Most of your aims and objectives are reasonable and you should find a little luck coming your way. Your confidence is not lacking and you can afford some cautious speculation during today and tomorrow, but never gamble more than you can afford to lose.

25 MONDAY   *Moon Age Day 21*   *Moon Sign Scorpio*

When it comes to getting things done, and to having your own way, today should turn out to be ideal in every respect. Since the charming side of your nature is even more on display than usual, it is unlikely that anyone will refuse reasonable requests. Competition is strong at work but you are equal to the task.

26 TUESDAY   *Moon Age Day 22*   *Moon Sign Sagittarius*

You will now enjoy the stimulation that can come from travel and the fact that the year is so new and that the winter weather may be at its worst does little to put you off. You need a change of scenery and it doesn't really matter where you choose to go. If you avoid the issue you may well be left feeling downhearted.

27 WEDNESDAY   *Moon Age Day 23*   *Moon Sign Sagittarius*

Learning experiences remain pleasurable and offer you the chance to see yourself in a very different light. It might occur to you that much of what has been happening recently has had a slightly selfish aspect to it. This could be true but even your caring zodiac sign is allowed to be a little selfish sometimes.

28 THURSDAY   *Moon Age Day 24*   *Moon Sign Sagittarius*

Personal relationships may be somewhat more troublesome today than has been the case of late. Your partner could prove to be emotionally demanding and you won't have all the answers to the problems that family members are posing. Part of the reason for this is a negative attitude on your part.

March 2019

1 FRIDAY
Moon Age Day 25   Moon Sign Capricorn

Progress in your career may be easy to achieve under current trends. There are people around who can be extremely useful to you, but this is a two-way street and you will offer them some timely assistance in return. You are probably in for a busy day but since it seems that it will be generally successful, the time should pass quickly and happily.

2 SATURDAY
Moon Age Day 26   Moon Sign Capricorn

Along comes a period during which you will be broadening your horizons quite successfully. Don't get involved in shady deals of any sort, particularly with people you cannot trust instinctively. An early start to the day would mean more time to please yourself later, something that is quite important.

3 SUNDAY
Moon Age Day 27   Moon Sign Aquarius

What a good time this is for entertaining new ideas, specifically ones that are going to help you get ahead in a financial sense later. There may be some interesting moments romantically, or just possibly regarding a new friendship, together with a slightly more solid time on the financial front.

4 MONDAY
Moon Age Day 28   Moon Sign Aquarius

Home comforts have a special appeal now, probably because you are tending to shy away from the wider world to a certain extent. This isn't so unusual. Your zodiac sign is often committed to the place where you feel most secure. Paradoxically, you might also feel the need to travel around this time.

5 TUESDAY *Moon Age Day 29   Moon Sign Aquarius*

There is certainly no doubting your loyalty at present, nor your commitment to people who have looked after you in the past. Finding time to do what pleases you personally will be quite difficult today, but since you are probably on the go from morning until night, this might not occur to you until later.

6 WEDNESDAY ☿ *Moon Age Day 0   Moon Sign Pisces*

This is not a good time to be involved in conflict with either colleagues or friends. You are going to get on much better if you create a harmonious atmosphere, but bear in mind that you don't have to subjugate your own wishes to do so. It is possible to be diplomatic but firm, and garner respect as a result.

7 THURSDAY ☿ *Moon Age Day 1   Moon Sign Pisces*

There are some very grateful people around now, perhaps because of things you have done for them recently. They are likely to show their gratitude in a number of different ways, all of which should please you. This may not be a day for too many adventures, but small ones can be fun.

8 FRIDAY ☿ *Moon Age Day 2   Moon Sign Aries*

Your ego could be bruised today, especially if you take on any big tasks. Keep life light and even, that way you won't be disappointed. In a personal sense, you can expect more attention to be coming your way any time now, which may lead to a fairly interesting time for some Scorpios.

9 SATURDAY ☿ *Moon Age Day 3   Moon Sign Aries*

Some hopeful news arrives this weekend, enlivening things no end. You are in the mood for excitement and will want to help others have a good time as well. Your confidence is generally high and you have a great desire to ring the changes in one way or another, specifically with regard to travel.

10 SUNDAY ☿ *Moon Age Day 4   Moon Sign Taurus*

It is important to layoff between important activities, simply to have a rest. By all means get on with something simple, and which doesn't tax your mind too much. You need moments to daydream, which are important to all of us. Casual conversations can have far reaching implications.

11 MONDAY ☿ *Moon Age Day 5   Moon Sign Taurus*

Avoid pushing yourself too hard today. The lunar low is around and you should be far enough ahead in a general sense not to have to rush. Take time out to look, to think and to plan. Personal attachments should be sound and could offer you a warm glow when you need it the most.

12 TUESDAY ☿ *Moon Age Day 6   Moon Sign Taurus*

Don't be taken in too easily by the tales others are telling. Many of these will be distorted, or downright wrong. It is better, for the moment, to judge by your own intuition, which is strong today. Some of your conclusions might be said to verge on the 'psychic' because they are so accurate.

13 WEDNESDAY ☿ *Moon Age Day 7   Moon Sign Gemini*

You should be on generally good form and can make a splash in social situations today. Although you could be somewhat quieter than yesterday, you still get the message across, and do so with great charm. Contradictions are possible in your working life and you will have to deal with these one at a time if they arise.

14 THURSDAY ☿ *Moon Age Day 8   Moon Sign Gemini*

Professional issues will find you making the best of yourself today. For the first time this year, it could occur to you that spring is just around the corner, a state of affairs that should cheer you up no end. Romantically and personally it appears that you are on very good form.

15 FRIDAY ☿ *Moon Age Day 9 Moon Sign Cancer*

You can spend so much time in search of fresh ideas and places to go, that nothing much gets done today, but does it matter? This is a time when you will want to please yourself and you cannot be available for everyone else all the time. There is no real change in the positive face you are showing to the world.

16 SATURDAY ☿ *Moon Age Day 10 Moon Sign Cancer*

Make use of some subtle tactics at present. When it comes to getting what you want, you can be second to none and have a great ability to persuade others that your point of view is the right one. Don't be too quick to jump to conclusions in matters relating to love.

17 SUNDAY ☿ *Moon Age Day 11 Moon Sign Cancer*

Not everything you want is going to turn out right but you do have the ability to capitalise on those situations in which you know you can succeed. Routine matters may become exciting and the most mundane of relationships have lots to offer today. Give yourself a break from something you hate.

18 MONDAY ☿ *Moon Age Day 12 Moon Sign Leo*

This is a time during which it will be vitally important to keep personal comments out of diplomatic discussions. Try not to get too hung up on details and do yourself a favour in terms of finances by taking money that is clearly being offered. Someone you haven't seen for ages could make a return to your life.

19 TUESDAY ☿ *Moon Age Day 13 Moon Sign Leo*

Things undertaken with friends or as part of a group take on a good feel as you co-operate well with others. Good friends you haven't seen for some time may pay you a visit and even general gossip is of interest to you right now. Plan a journey today, even if it won't take place for months.

20 WEDNESDAY ☿ *Moon Age Day 14* *Moon Sign Virgo*

You get the best from life now if you mix and mingle with as many different people as you can. Arrangements for travel could present the odd problem but in the main you are funny, easy to talk to and great to have around. If words of love come your way later in the day, believe what is being said.

21 THURSDAY ☿ *Moon Age Day 15* *Moon Sign Virgo*

Your common sense cuts in now and you may decide to slow things down. You want to find the time to tell certain people how you feel and that's exactly what you can do today. Give yourself a pat on the back for a recent success but don't get too complacent. There is plenty to be done in the days ahead.

22 FRIDAY ☿ *Moon Age Day 16* *Moon Sign Libra*

A positive focus on career developments helps to take your mind off slightly negative trends in other directions. The end of the working week will offer you the chance to plan ahead towards a weekend that can offer significant rewards. You could be feeling romantic by evening.

23 SATURDAY ☿ *Moon Age Day 17* *Moon Sign Libra*

It would be far better to think matters through carefully now, rather than rushing at stopgap measures. When it comes to major decisions that have a bearing on the longer-term aspects of life you could do worse than to seek the help and support of friends who knows you very well.

24 SUNDAY ☿ *Moon Age Day 18* *Moon Sign Scorpio*

You should be reaching quite a peak now. The lunar high is strong in your chart, leading to a chattier disposition on your part, and perhaps also bringing better luck. Although you won't want to speculate too much, it's a fact that your hunches are strong and your ability to win through quite marked.

25 MONDAY ☿ *Moon Age Day 19   Moon Sign Scorpio*

This is another day that appears to be geared, fundamentally, towards personal success. You are chattier than usual, and willing to put your point of view to just about anyone who is willing to listen. This means superiors too and the impression you make will not be wasted.

26 TUESDAY ☿ *Moon Age Day 20   Moon Sign Sagittarius*

You may have to deal with a few difficult emotional issues today. Try not to react too strongly if you feel that others are behaving irrationally. From their point of view, it is likely that you are also acting oddly. All that's required is a little patience on the part of all concerned.

27 WEDNESDAY ☿ *Moon Age Day 21   Moon Sign Sagittarius*

It could be hard to put your finger on potential sources of tension at the moment. They may well have something to do with your own restlessness. This is a time when you really could do with some travel, though everyday requirements are likely to prevent that from being a realistic possibility.

28 THURSDAY ☿ *Moon Age Day 22   Moon Sign Capricorn*

You could do worse today than to find yourself somewhere new and unusual to go. There are plenty of possibilities and the more you think about it, the greater are your options. You are only likely to encounter a problem if you try to do everything at once, a course of action that is very likely to lead to failure and disappointment.

29 FRIDAY *Moon Age Day 23   Moon Sign Capricorn*

This is a day during which material acquisitions seem to come straight to you as and when you need them. Some of this could be as a result of the assistance on offer from others, especially as you are particularly affectionate at this time, but some of it may be simply down to your own hard work.

30 SATURDAY   *Moon Age Day 24   Moon Sign Capricorn*

It should be easy to find a warm welcome wherever you choose to go today. The weekend strengthens your desire for social activity with others. Spending long periods on your own is not to be recommended at present, and neither is backing off when things don't go your way.

31 SUNDAY   *Moon Age Day 25   Moon Sign Aquarius*

Socially speaking you continue on the up and people who you get along well with should surround you. Ignore entreaties from loved ones to behave in the way they would wish. It's really important to be yourself at this stage of the month.

April

2019

1 MONDAY
Moon Age Day 26   Moon Sign Aquarius

You could be at serious loggerheads with someone regarding a personal matter today. Even though disagreement is never ideal, in this case it would probably be better to talk things through than to keep silent on the issue. Harbouring resentment isn't good for anyone, but especially not for sensitive Scorpios.

2 TUESDAY
Moon Age Day 27   Moon Sign Pisces

You can get a great deal from professional matters today, as you enter an excellent period for working Scorpios. Don't be inclined to hold back if someone thinks they know better than you. Their judgement is probably subjective and, since you are a deep thinker, you may have the intellectual and moral high ground.

3 WEDNESDAY
Moon Age Day 28   Moon Sign Pisces

A friend could turn out to be something of a letdown today. This is part of life. You are extremely loyal and tend to expect everyone to be the same, but often they are not. Try not to entertain unreasonable expectations of people and you are less likely to be disappointed.

4 THURSDAY
Moon Age Day 29   Moon Sign Pisces

You might have to make a few sacrifices in your relationship in order to keep up with a much more frenetic professional and practical pace of life. Although you may be subdued, you have a good ability to get your message across to others today. Sporting activities look likely to lead to success.

93

5 FRIDAY
Moon Age Day 0   Moon Sign Aries

The events of today can bring strong emotions to the surface. It's possible that some circumstances are more promising for you than they first appeared. Spreading a particular series of jobs across the day might seem sensible, but once you get started you might decide to do everything in one go.

6 SATURDAY
Moon Age Day 1   Moon Sign Aries

A beneficial phase for your career and for your long-term plans begins today. You should be feeling confident, especially when you are going in directions that you clearly understand. Trends suggest that you are likely to encounter other Scorpios around now.

7 SUNDAY
Moon Age Day 2   Moon Sign Taurus

As the lunar low appears, your spirits might be flagging a little. Prepare for delays and for your movement to be somehow curtailed. Remember, though, that no planetary aspect can prevent you from thinking and planning. Spending today in contemplation should pay dividends later.

8 MONDAY
Moon Age Day 3   Moon Sign Taurus

This might be a good time to keep a low profile. There really isn't anything to be gained today by interfering in any matter, and arguments are definitely to be avoided. Personal relationships ought to offer a degree of satisfaction, though material progress might be more or less denied until tomorrow.

9 TUESDAY
Moon Age Day 4   Moon Sign Gemini

Your main achievement today will come from group endeavours and events that throw you together with large numbers of people. Even casual acquaintances may have some interesting news to impart and there is always the chance that someone you haven't known well in the past could become a loyal friend.

10 WEDNESDAY   *Moon Age Day 5   Moon Sign Gemini*

You tend to show a very self-sacrificing face to the world today. This isn't so strange for Scorpio because your concern for others is legendary. If you have a job that involves commitment to other people, you ought to be able to express yourself quite fully. Isolationist tendencies must be avoided at all costs.

11 THURSDAY   *Moon Age Day 6   Moon Sign Gemini*

In terms of social encounters, the more the merrier is the rule for today. Still quite willing to join in with the fun, you should be popular and well able to make an impression. There is just a chance that not everyone will find you wonderful, but nobody can have everything!

12 FRIDAY   *Moon Age Day 7   Moon Sign Cancer*

Rewarding experiences through friendship are now more likely than ever. Things may not be exactly exciting at the moment, but your imagination is working well and you can easily help to pep things up in your vicinity. What you definitely have is popularity, and that isn't bad for starters.

13 SATURDAY   *Moon Age Day 8   Moon Sign Cancer*

Trends indicate disputes, both at home and at work. Try to keep away from them if you can. A degree of wanderlust is also indicated in your chart, so if the spring weather is enticing, take the opportunity to get out of the house and blow away the cobwebs. You might actively choose to spend time with friends.

14 SUNDAY   *Moon Age Day 9   Moon Sign Leo*

Let go and express yourself today. Many planetary positions around you at the moment suggest that you are talking fluently and with conviction. You shouldn't have any trouble at all getting others to listen to what you are saying, and they won't misconstrue the message.

15 MONDAY
Moon Age Day 10   Moon Sign Leo

Your approach to a particular issue could be a little unrealistic under current trends, and as a result, you may be thrown in your judgement. On the whole, though, today should be light hearted and a time to enjoy what life has in store for you.

16 TUESDAY
Moon Age Day 11   Moon Sign Virgo

Expect a few stresses in relationships today. The best way to avoid these is to keep things light and open. Deep and meaningful conversations are probably not the best way to move forward at present. On a positive note, there could be a little more cash about than you had expected.

17 WEDNESDAY
Moon Age Day 12   Moon Sign Virgo

Professional advancement comes along as a result of who rather than what you know. Keep your eyes open now because you may get the opportunity to impress certain people, some of whom are in a position to help you out. Your approach to life is now less likely to be clouded by so much deep thinking.

18 THURSDAY
Moon Age Day 13   Moon Sign Libra

You might have to pay attention to something that is no longer a part of your own life and this can seem a bother because you want to look ahead right now. Don't be too quick to judge the way others are behaving, particularly family members. Finally, there is really no need to rush your fences at present.

19 FRIDAY
Moon Age Day 14   Moon Sign Libra

It is true that there are certain obstacles to be overcome and life can seem complicated as a result. This should not be too much of a problem as long as you maintain a healthy sense of humour and don't allow issues to get on top of you. There are friends on whom you can rely, most likely later in the day.

20 SATURDAY   *Moon Age Day 15   Moon Sign Scorpio*

Now you are really on top form and will make the most of anything that life puts in your path. Sharp, intelligent and perceptive, you can thank the lunar high for your capability on every level. You might particularly enjoy a journey planned at short notice.

21 SUNDAY   *Moon Age Day 16   Moon Sign Scorpio*

Getting your own way ought to be a piece of cake today. This is a good way to spend Sunday, with lots of energy and a real determination to get things done. If you start early, you can keep ahead of the game, and still have plenty of oomph left for the evening. Social trends look especially good.

22 MONDAY   *Moon Age Day 17   Moon Sign Sagittarius*

A boost to matters that have a social aspect ought to be obvious around now, together with a real determination on your part to show your own worth. The beginning of this new week offers unexpected incentives and brings you to a better understanding of your position at work and within the family.

23 TUESDAY   *Moon Age Day 18   Moon Sign Sagittarius*

It is true that life has its ups and downs, but you are in a good position to deal with both rationally and with common sense. If there are disputes at work, it is up to you to pour oil on troubled water. Even undertaking jobs you dislike should not be at all difficult.

24 WEDNESDAY   *Moon Age Day 19   Moon Sign Capricorn*

Today you could need some special help to get out of a jam, even though the problem is one that owes nothing to your own decisions or past actions. If you explain yourself to the right people, there is every reason to believe they can reverse difficult situations. Much of life is a state of mind at present.

25 THURSDAY
Moon Age Day 20   Moon Sign Capricorn

Social matters and teamwork situations are where your most rewarding moments are to be found right now. Someone is filled with admiration regarding the way you have dealt with a specific issue and it looks as though you are going to be number one in their books at least.

26 FRIDAY
Moon Age Day 21   Moon Sign Capricorn

Your home life should be very busy as the weekend approaches, probably because your family members have a greater need of your help and support. Don't allow circumstances to run you and – even if it means overturning thoughts and feelings that have been present for years – remember you are in charge.

27 SATURDAY
Moon Age Day 22   Moon Sign Aquarius

If you are a weekend worker, you can expect professional relationships to be great fun and to offer significant potential rewards. For Scorpios who are at home this Saturday, there is a real need to change the record domestically. Get out of the house if you possibly can and find ways to see issues differently.

28 SUNDAY
Moon Age Day 23   Moon Sign Aquarius

Looking at life through the eyes of other people has never been easier and this can prove to be a tremendous gift. Don't worry about the somewhat offhand attitude of a particular friend. They are going through a rather hard time and could be inclined to lash out at those they care for the most.

29 MONDAY
Moon Age Day 24   Moon Sign Pisces

You have powerful feelings today and will not be afraid to make them known. A quite voluble and emotionally inspired Scorpio is something the world doesn't see every day, so you are bound to receive a good deal of attention. A new month comes along in a couple of days and you will want to prepare yourself for it somehow.

30 TUESDAY

Moon Age Day 25   Moon Sign Pisces

The things that others are saying have a great bearing on the way you think today. Although you are not likely to become depressed at this time, you are inclined to dig deep inside that fathomless mind of yours. If this gives others the impression you are down in the dumps you will want to reassure them this is not the case.

May

2019

1 WEDNESDAY
Moon Age Day 26   Moon Sign Pisces

A boost to a family matter should come along at any time now. Make sure you begin today with a very positive attitude and a definite desire to succeed. If not everything goes your way at first, you can at least rely on the support of some very willing friends, plus, perhaps, your life partner.

2 THURSDAY
Moon Age Day 27   Moon Sign Aries

It feels good to be in the middle of a group today, maintaining a position at the centre of anything that is happening in your vicinity. Some Scorpios will now be thinking in terms of a new job, or consolidation with regard to the current one. You should get a warm reception from everyone around you.

3 FRIDAY
Moon Age Day 28   Moon Sign Aries

There could be a few mishaps now, especially in the workplace. You need to take some extra care and utilise the famous Scorpio common sense. Don't be at all worried if you have to tell someone else to take life more steadily, because whether they like it or not you are doing them a favour.

4 SATURDAY
Moon Age Day 0   Moon Sign Taurus

There could be intimate issues to deal with today. If you take these too seriously there is a chance they could get you down, which is not to be recommended. Maybe you ought to avoid dealing with anything too deep at the moment, opting instead to take a general overview of life, and all its various hues.

5 SUNDAY
Moon Age Day 1   Moon Sign Taurus

Things on the work front can become rather sluggish, so all the better if you don't work at the weekend. The lunar low keeps life slightly less exciting than you might wish, although you can pep it up somewhat if you make the effort. Listen to family members, some of whom have an important message to impart.

6 MONDAY
Moon Age Day 2   Moon Sign Taurus

Contradictions can be the order of the day. Just when you think people around you are happy, you might discover that they are not. Let's face it, the trends are not brilliant today, and you would be better spending at least a little time on your own. By tomorrow, the sky will look clearer and the way ahead less misty.

7 TUESDAY
Moon Age Day 3   Moon Sign Gemini

There is vital information around and you wouldn't want to miss it. For this reason alone you should keep your ears and eyes firmly open today. It will be clear to you that not everyone you come across is telling the truth. If this is the case, you will have to use your intuition in order to establish what is really going on.

8 WEDNESDAY
Moon Age Day 4   Moon Sign Gemini

Though your aims and objectives are generally on target today, there could be the odd frustration, caused in the main by not understanding exactly what those around you are really saying, especially at work. Once again, tune in that Scorpio mind and simply listen to what is being said.

9 THURSDAY
Moon Age Day 5   Moon Sign Cancer

You may fare better with solo endeavours today, and will relish the chance to act without consultation with others. Wanting to be on your own from time to time is certainly no novelty to the Scorpion. Such periods merely allow you to clear your mind and to meditate about recent events.

10 FRIDAY   *Moon Age Day 6   Moon Sign Cancer*

You are now ready to make concessions to others, even people who have clearly messed you about in the recent past. That doesn't mean you are knuckling under in any way, something you would hate to do under present planetary trends. In fact, what you are actually doing is establishing compromise.

11 SATURDAY   *Moon Age Day 7   Moon Sign Leo*

New trends come along and now you may feel your influence on the outside world to be lacking at present. As a result, you are hesitant and inclined to ask others for their opinions before you act. It isn't at all clear whether you will receive answers that please you, in which case it might be better to keep your own counsel in the first place.

12 SUNDAY   *Moon Age Day 8   Moon Sign Leo*

Your persuasive powers are limited today, but by inverse proportion, your natural scepticism is stronger. This ought to be a generally happy, although unremarkable time. Friendships feel supportive and there are likely to be some new people coming into your life.

13 MONDAY   *Moon Age Day 9   Moon Sign Virgo*

You are now quite susceptible to the influence of others. This is fine, just as long as you know and trust the people you are listening to. There is a sort of waver this week in your ability to sort the wheat from the chaff. Only a deep look into both intuition and common sense will reveal the answers you need.

14 TUESDAY   *Moon Age Day 10   Moon Sign Virgo*

Your home life could certainly seem like an area of release from practical and professional pressures right now. Be willing to relax, and don't take on any more jobs around the house than are absolutely necessary. The exception here might be tasks you genuinely enjoy.

15 WEDNESDAY *Moon Age Day 11   Moon Sign Libra*

Today shows that personal and romantic issues are working out far better than they have of late and, in the main, to your satisfaction. The focus is definitely on your love life and there are also small financial gains to be made, probably in part because you are willing to take a little chance.

16 THURSDAY *Moon Age Day 12   Moon Sign Libra*

Ensuring that you are properly in the know regarding things that are happening around you at the moment is very important. Don't be too quick to jump to unnecessary conclusions, especially regarding the way others are behaving. There are some small financial gains possible.

17 FRIDAY *Moon Age Day 13   Moon Sign Scorpio*

Now you can afford to dispense with caution and take life by the scruff of the neck. Today ought to be bright, cheerful and full of exciting events. If it doesn't look as though things are going to turn out that way of their own accord, then make it happen. This is not a time to be a wallflower or to hang back in any way.

18 SATURDAY *Moon Age Day 14   Moon Sign Scorpio*

Your energy level is still at a peak so prepare for an eventful Saturday. You are now more likely to be focused on your own desires and less on those of others. Footloose and fancy free as you are, perhaps you should not be too surprised at some of the romantic attention that is coming your way.

19 SUNDAY *Moon Age Day 15   Moon Sign Scorpio*

Getting out and about should be easier now for two reasons: you have more time on your hands and your finances ought to be a little better than of late. Don't be held back by people who don't really have any better idea how to proceed than you, even if they pretend they do.

20 MONDAY *Moon Age Day 16   Moon Sign Sagittarius*

You can gain a great deal from simply talking things over today, partly because you are surrounded by people who are so reasonable and who are willing to give you a fair hearing. At work there are potential gains in terms of the responsibilities you will be expected to take on for the future.

21 TUESDAY *Moon Age Day 17   Moon Sign Sagittarius*

It is extremely important to you at the moment that you are liked. That's fine and it is part of the person you are but you can't expect everyone to think you are flavour of the month. Going to extremes to bring someone on side who just doesn't understand the way you tick is a waste of energy.

22 WEDNESDAY *Moon Age Day 18   Moon Sign Capricorn*

A complete change of scene would suit you down to the ground now. Even if this is not possible you can at least ring the changes in one way or another. Those amongst you who have decided on a holiday this early in the year could have made a very sensible decision. It is a break from routine you need the most.

23 THURSDAY *Moon Age Day 19   Moon Sign Capricorn*

Your ability to communicate with your partner may not be so great at present, and if this is the case, a third party mediator might be necessary. All in all, this shouldn't be a bad day but it could prove rather tedious unless you allow yourself the opportunity to break from day-to-day routines in some way.

24 FRIDAY *Moon Age Day 20   Moon Sign Aquarius*

Trends alter a little, and now daily routines keep you nicely on the go, though you will find once again that there is probably very little to set this day apart and you may sometimes be a little bored. The answer lies in your own hands and is down to the amount of effort you choose to put in to ring the changes.

25 SATURDAY   *Moon Age Day 21   Moon Sign Aquarius*

Expect a low-key sort of day and one during which you may not have quite the impact on the world you would wish. The more you commit yourself to routine matters, the greater is the contentment you are likely to find. Scorpio is very thoughtful at present and this shows in most of what you do.

26 SUNDAY   *Moon Age Day 22   Moon Sign Aquarius*

There are matters close to your heart today that ought to be discussed with others. Getting to the bottom of a mystery is something else that appeals to you right now and your world could be filled with little puzzles of one sort or another. Your attention to detail is good and allows you to score some successes.

27 MONDAY   *Moon Age Day 23   Moon Sign Pisces*

The start of another working week finds you lively and sociable. There probably won't be anything extraordinary about today but it does have its positive moments, not least in love. Explaining the way you feel about anything on your mind right now brings you to a better understanding of yourself.

28 TUESDAY   *Moon Age Day 24   Moon Sign Pisces*

You need to avoid being sidetracked by matters that are of no real importance. There is a danger that you could fall between two stalls in the attitude you are taking to a particular issue, leaving you to doubt where your heart really lies. In sporting activities, this is clearly a time to get involved.

29 WEDNESDAY   *Moon Age Day 25   Moon Sign Aries*

There is just a slight tendency for you to overcomplicate issues that are not really difficult at all now. Try to remain on-track when it comes to your work, especially since you could be on the verge of advancement. What makes today quite important is the way others are watching your progress.

30 THURSDAY
Moon Age Day 26   Moon Sign Aries

You are at the peak of your powers today, both mentally and probably physically. This might lead you on a fitness regime or down the road to other improvements you think are necessary. It would be sensible to plan such matters carefully because there is a risk of you being a little impulsive at present.

31 FRIDAY
Moon Age Day 27   Moon Sign Aries

Trends suggest that not everything you hear from others should be believed at this time and it is possible that someone is trying to fool you in some way. Take any opportunities offered to you today and don't let anyone's unsolicited advice put you off.

June

2019

1 SATURDAY
Moon Age Day 28   Moon Sign Taurus

Since you are not likely to be pushing hard in a practical sense, the lunar low doesn't really restrict you very much this time around. This is an ideal time to plan a journey, or to decide that the time is right for alterations and changes on the domestic scene. Treat a friend today; you might even receive a gift yourself.

2 SUNDAY
Moon Age Day 29   Moon Sign Taurus

Make sure your desire to assert yourself doesn't get you into hot water today. All in all, a low-key approach to certain situations would work better than an aggressive one and should promote a more positive reaction from others. Your common sense will tell you when you need to tread softly.

3 MONDAY
Moon Age Day 0   Moon Sign Gemini

A personal issue which now seems rather up in the air could cause just a little consternation early in the day, though not for long if you deal with it quickly. Your confidence isn't lacking, even though finding something to do with it might not be very easy right now. Friends should be especially supportive.

4 TUESDAY
Moon Age Day 1   Moon Sign Gemini

A minor boost to career matters has the potential to lift your spirits no end right now. You have plenty of energy and a greater determination to push ahead, even if there are obstacles on the way. It might be necessary to resist the urge to travel today because there are too many jobs to be done.

5 WEDNESDAY   *Moon Age Day 2   Moon Sign Cancer*

A few disappointments are possible in your love life, but you could avoid these if you think and look ahead. When it comes to pleasing your partner you are, as always, willing to do anything you can. However, the demands that are made of you today might be excessive and could lead to some fatigue.

6 THURSDAY   *Moon Age Day 3   Moon Sign Cancer*

Try to avoid allowing personal matters to have a bearing on your performance in the outside world. If you are worrying about things, you won't be shining as much as you should. For this reason alone you should tackle any potential problem head on, and defuse it before it has the chance to throw you.

7 FRIDAY   *Moon Age Day 4   Moon Sign Leo*

You have many versatile skills just itching to be used today. With a good deal of joy coming into your life, you should be on top form, especially in personal and family relationships where your advice may be sought more and more. Trends also suggest that someone from the past may come back into your life.

8 SATURDAY   *Moon Age Day 5   Moon Sign Leo*

Influences happening today keep you in the social mainstream, and this looks likely to continue for a few days to come. Although there are occasions when you prefer your own space, right now this is a privilege you don't really have.

9 SUNDAY   *Moon Age Day 6   Moon Sign Virgo*

Despite your best efforts, you may struggle to be organised today. There are times when it is simply good to let others take some of the strain and this appears to be such a period for you. This is not to suggest you are choosing to take a back seat, merely that trends favour it for now.

10 MONDAY
Moon Age Day 7   Moon Sign Virgo

Trends move on, and your mind is sharp and clear today, which inclines you to look for swift answers to problems. Give and take is important in family matters, but you should have little difficulty in getting those around you on side. Friendly and affable you should be enjoying the social limelight.

11 TUESDAY
Moon Age Day 8   Moon Sign Virgo

You are always sympathetic towards others, but especially so today. Much of your time may be spent doing things for one person or another and you are a good listener when those around you need to talk. This is fine, but don't forget your own needs on the way.

12 WEDNESDAY
Moon Age Day 9   Moon Sign Libra

Unfinished business should be dealt with early in the day leaving more hours later to please yourself, which is what you really want to do most at present. Not everyone is on your side today, so take care that the few people who are do not fall foul of the sharp end of your intellect.

13 THURSDAY
Moon Age Day 10   Moon Sign Libra

You ought to be able to deal quite positively with an issue from the past that has been hanging over you for some time. This will lead to a lessening of unnecessary anxiety. There is much that is casual about today, but trends suggest that this merely hides some essential truths.

14 FRIDAY
Moon Age Day 11   Moon Sign Scorpio

The lunar high arrives and brings with it the one, certain period this month when you are able to push ahead on all fronts. Don't allow yourself to be held back or suppressed in any way. The moves you make under these trends should stay with you in a positive way for the remainder of the month at least.

15 SATURDAY *Moon Age Day 12   Moon Sign Scorpio*

This is a time of optimism and high spirits, which coincides at least partly with the weekend. You can be assertive when it is necessary, although trends suggest that you will not need to push your weight around with family members and friends. There is great scope for travel, both today and tomorrow.

16 SUNDAY *Moon Age Day 13   Moon Sign Sagittarius*

There is a degree of restlessness about at the moment and this means having to move around as freely as you can. It certainly won't be the sort of period during which you would relish being tied to the same spot and you would be happy to travel as much as possible. Avoid pointless routines today.

17 MONDAY *Moon Age Day 14   Moon Sign Sagittarius*

Trends governing your love life are on the up and you should turn heads wherever you go. Whether relationships are established or brand new, this is the time to get it on with the main person in your life. It is difficult to hide the sensual qualities of your Water-sign nature at this time, no matter how hard you try.

18 TUESDAY *Moon Age Day 15   Moon Sign Capricorn*

Effective communication could lead you to score significant points at present. If there are jobs about that you don't like the look of, get them out of the way as early in the day as you can. Any discomfort caused by minor health problems should diminish quickly.

19 WEDNESDAY *Moon Age Day 16   Moon Sign Capricorn*

Despite the fact that it may appear today as though things are not really going your way, keep your eye on the future and plan ahead. By tomorrow, more positive trends are on the way and you should be fully up to speed. Keep away from negative types and make your own decisions.

20 THURSDAY   *Moon Age Day 17   Moon Sign Capricorn*

Something you have been waiting for may now work out the way you wanted. Your patience and persistence has paid off. Your general affability means that few will deny you your moment of glory and anyone awkward is not worth considering now.

21 FRIDAY   *Moon Age Day 18   Moon Sign Aquarius*

Don't try to do too much today. Those things that are clearly in view are the ones that count the most and you won't help yourself if you push harder than you know is necessary. Confidence is one thing, but blind faith is something completely different. A good day for coming to terms with wayward friends.

22 SATURDAY   *Moon Age Day 19   Moon Sign Aquarius*

In the recent past you might have found it rather more difficult than usual to get through to those who are generally close to you. This situation is about to change. They come to realise how deep your sincerity actually runs and could therefore be all the more willing to tell you a few of their secrets.

23 SUNDAY   *Moon Age Day 20   Moon Sign Pisces*

Your Sunday can be filled with promise, plus a good deal of excitement if you are in the market for it. It might not be easy to conform to expectations but you are so good to know that people may not worry about this. On the contrary, your unorthodox way of doing things at present appeals the most.

24 MONDAY   *Moon Age Day 21   Moon Sign Pisces*

The desire to get ahead could push you to do things you might otherwise shy away from. Continue to be positive and to display the strong level of confidence that impresses others so much. However, a certain amount of caution is indicated, particularly when it comes to close, personal encounters.

25 TUESDAY   *Moon Age Day 22   Moon Sign Pisces*

Now is the time for fast thinking and instant action. If you are quick off the mark you can make progress in a number of different directions and might gain quite a reputation on the way. Scorpios who are self employed might be the luckiest of all under present circumstances.

26 WEDNESDAY   *Moon Age Day 23   Moon Sign Aries*

Don't take anything too seriously today because there are plenty of jokers around – in fact you may be the biggest one of all. Get out and about if you can because a journey would suit you down to the ground. Even a holiday isn't out of the question.

27 THURSDAY   *Moon Age Day 24   Moon Sign Aries*

What a great time this is to get new plans out in the open and working for you. Friends and relatives alike should be only too willing to lend a hand, especially because your personality is so bubbly now. Getting on with just about anyone proves to be as easy as pie.

28 FRIDAY   *Moon Age Day 25   Moon Sign Taurus*

Put a brake on ambitions at this stage of the week. For the next two days the lunar low is going to slow you down so there is no point in fighting against the odds. Instead, do what you can to enjoy yourself and be ready for Sunday, when the situation improves.

29 SATURDAY   *Moon Age Day 26   Moon Sign Taurus*

This really is not one of the luckiest days of the month for you. Although you can't alter this fact, you can mitigate its effect by not putting yourself in the way of too many risks. Before you volunteer for anything, ask yourself if you really should be doing so at all. Take extra care in all areas until tomorrow.

30 SUNDAY
Moon Age Day 27   Moon Sign Gemini

Make sure that others don't get the wrong end of the stick regarding your opinions. If you are too reticent, people could draw their own conclusions and there could be occasions when this is the last thing you want. It's also important to keep your eyes open for new and renewed professional opportunities.

July

2019

1 MONDAY
Moon Age Day 28   Moon Sign Gemini

You might be looking for more support and favours from your partner than you are receiving right now. Things at home could therefore be a little strained, and your mood may not help matters. However, you should have plenty of confidence for social matters so get out and about if you need to take a break.

2 TUESDAY
Moon Age Day 0   Moon Sign Gemini

Avoid being too impulsive in financial matters and save some money for later. You may have to get up early today in order to get everything necessary done and out of the way. This is important because later in the day you will want to do what takes your fancy.

3 WEDNESDAY
Moon Age Day 1   Moon Sign Cancer

You should enjoy the maximum amount of energy and vitality right now, so much so that you might need to curb your enthusiasm before you run out of steam. The quiet Scorpion is now taking a holiday and you will want to have your say, no matter what sort of company you are in.

4 THURSDAY
Moon Age Day 2   Moon Sign Cancer

You are not quite as strong today as seems to have been the case yesterday. Emotionally speaking you might be in a bit of a mess, probably on account of something that ought not to worry you at all. A good cry on the shoulder of a friend may all it takes to get you over this period, and you should be laughing again soon enough.

5 FRIDAY *Moon Age Day 3   Moon Sign Leo*

It isn't too late to put your luck to the test, though you would be better keeping such efforts to the morning. You are able to talk to just about anyone about a variety of subjects this Friday and it appears that any shyness in your personality has vanished. This isn't true of course, but it certainly doesn't show right now.

6 SATURDAY *Moon Age Day 4   Moon Sign Leo*

There might be a chance of a profitable development at work and finances generally ought to look stronger around the start of the weekend. You may need to find a compromise when dealing with younger family members, some of whom could prove to be in an awkward frame of mind.

7 SUNDAY *Moon Age Day 5   Moon Sign Virgo*

You should be a lively presence on the social scene this Sunday, and will certainly be enjoying the warm days and friendly, out-of-doors evenings. Avoid confrontations with your partner or someone else who is special to you. It certainly will not do you any good at all to lose your temper.

8 MONDAY ☿ *Moon Age Day 6   Moon Sign Virgo*

Hang fire before pushing ahead with specific plans or one particular scheme that has been on your mind. Don't be tempted to worry about problems before they have materialised and simply deal with the needs of the day one at a time. Most people around you appear to have your best interests at heart and so should prove helpful.

9 TUESDAY ☿ *Moon Age Day 7   Moon Sign Libra*

It could be that you have your work cut out for you, keeping on top of material concerns. The strange thing is that most of them could quite easily take care of themselves but you feel a need to tinker with them right now. Avoid confusion in relationships by speaking your mind in a no-nonsense way.

10 WEDNESDAY ☿   *Moon Age Day 8*   *Moon Sign Libra*

Right now you feel like doing something to please yourself, rather than running around assisting others all the time. You are perfectly entitled to put yourself first once in a while and you ought to be able to expect just a little support. If it isn't forthcoming, have a word in the right ear.

11 THURSDAY ☿   *Moon Age Day 9*   *Moon Sign Scorpio*

With the lunar high comes a mass of energy and an almost insatiable desire to find fresh fields and pastures new. There are activities in store that ought to keep you extremely happy, and maybe a gift from a more or less completely unexpected direction. Stay away from people who want to complicate your life, they will only spoil your mood.

12 FRIDAY ☿   *Moon Age Day 10*   *Moon Sign Scorpio*

Yesterday's favourable trends continue apace. Now you want to tell certain people how you feel about them, and generally speaking this should be in a very positive way. Someone you haven't seen for a long time could easily be making a renewed appearance in your life, and they may bring some surprising news with them.

13 SATURDAY ☿ *Moon Age Day 11*   *Moon Sign Sagittarius*

You almost certainly need more excitement than you can find at home this weekend. Although you are a home-bird for much of the year, it is around now that you feel a definite desire to get out into the countryside, or even more beneficially, to the coast. All you have to do is persuade someone to go with you.

14 SUNDAY ☿ *Moon Age Day 12*   *Moon Sign Sagittarius*

Though your sympathies are easily stirred today, you won't be able to help everyone out. Just bear in mind that a good deed each day is something you tend to do all the time. Friends might be seeking your special support but it may be necessary to tell at least some of them there is nothing you can do to help just for the moment.

15 MONDAY ☿ *Moon Age Day 13   Moon Sign Capricorn*

Minor challenges and even confrontations can be expected at work, which means you have to put on a good show in order to hold your own. But every good Scorpio knows that there is more than one way to skin a cat. Turn the intuition up to full, stay cool and wait for the appropriate moment.

16 TUESDAY ☿ *Moon Age Day 14   Moon Sign Capricorn*

Trends suggest that you can make great gains at work, particularly since you are presently willing to take the sort of chances you would have shied away from only a short time ago. The attitude of your family and friends presently makes it that much easier to gain their trust and co-operation in anything.

17 WEDNESDAY ☿ *Moon Age Day 15   Moon Sign Capricorn*

Don't miss out on any important news that is going around at present. This is a very sociable day and a time during which you will be happy to spend a few hours chatting with those you know and like the best. Good fortune is likely to follow your footsteps across the next few days.

18 THURSDAY ☿ *Moon Age Day 16   Moon Sign Aquarius*

Getting what you want from others and from specific situations now appears to be that much easier than it sometimes is. The shy and retiring side of the sign of Scorpio takes a holiday around now as you push forward with new incentives and with a confidence that others could possibly find quite astonishing in your case.

19 FRIDAY ☿ *Moon Age Day 17   Moon Sign Aquarius*

Over half way through the month and you still haven't done some of the things that seemed important right back at the end of June. Now is the time to assess the way situations are unfolding and to offer the extra assistance that is going to be necessary to get new plans off the drawing board and make them into reality.

20 SATURDAY ☿ *Moon Age Day 18* *Moon Sign Pisces*

This is a period that assists you to focus your mind more clearly than you have been able to for several months. Although your day is likely to be extremely busy you are able to let those around you know how important they are to you and just what their assistance in your life really means.

21 SUNDAY ☿ *Moon Age Day 19* *Moon Sign Pisces*

You feel energetic and strong, which is why you could be so adventurous at present. You may even be surprised at your own tenacity and bravery, leading you to little adventures you can really enjoy. Not everyone seems to be on your side at present, though the most important people will be.

22 MONDAY ☿ *Moon Age Day 20* *Moon Sign Pisces*

Daily life should have plenty to keep you both occupied and interested at the beginning of a new and mainly active week. Rules and regulations are easy to deal with – you will simply ignore them if they get in your way. Not everyone is going to be co-operative now so stick to those who are.

23 TUESDAY ☿ *Moon Age Day 21* *Moon Sign Aries*

There are some promising financial developments about and you will want to make the most of them when you can. Keep an eye open for opportunities that mean new investments, especially those that will provide for the more distant future. Romance is well starred in your chart today, so try to spend some time with your partner if you can.

24 WEDNESDAY ☿ *Moon Age Day 22* *Moon Sign Aries*

The drive to accomplish almost anything is stepped up markedly under present planetary trends. Don't hold back. This is a time to let everyone know what your strengths and capabilities are. Routines won't be very appealing on a day when new incentives count for the most.

25 THURSDAY ☿ *Moon Age Day 23   Moon Sign Taurus*

Although life is quieter now that the Moon is in your opposite zodiac sign, it could also feel a good deal more comfortable, at least in some ways. You won't have to think too hard at the moment and are willing to put some concerns to one side. By the time you go back to them, they might have disappeared.

26 FRIDAY ☿ *Moon Age Day 24   Moon Sign Taurus*

It could easily feel as if others are getting ahead a good deal faster than you are, and this is actually the case, but only for the moment. Look ahead, plan, and make the most of social prospects, which remain good. By the evening, you may be feeling more like your old self and therefore seeking out company.

27 SATURDAY ☿ *Moon Age Day 25   Moon Sign Taurus*

In a professional sense it is clear that you want to speak your mind, though this might be either difficult or impossible on a Saturday. If you are not a weekend worker, concentrate instead on things you have wanted to do in and around your home. Routine can prove to be your ally today.

28 SUNDAY ☿ *Moon Age Day 26   Moon Sign Gemini*

There can be a strong sense of nostalgia around at this time, leading you to spend as much time today looking back as you do forward. This contrasts markedly with your desire to get ahead and so you may feel a little in conflict with yourself. Resolve these issues by talking about them with someone you trust to help you work them through.

29 MONDAY ☿ *Moon Age Day 27   Moon Sign Gemini*

The pursuit of practical matters offers a greater chance of success than spending hours thinking things through. Yesterday was the time for consideration, while now is the moment to strike. There should be people around to assist you when you require it, though you might have to ask.

30 TUESDAY ☿ *Moon Age Day 28   Moon Sign Cancer*

Your acquisitive streak is definitely on display and you also know full well how to get money this week. Although you are rarely obsessed with material things, you are likely to be so to a greater extent now. Acting on impulse seems attractive but might not pay too many dividends at present so exercise some caution.

31 WEDNESDAY ☿ *Moon Age Day 0   Moon Sign Cancer*

An extra bit of effort in any situation really counts for a great deal at this time, which is why you are likely to be willing to march forward with determination, even though you could worry about some matters. Those you work with should prove to be reliable and supportive.

♏ August 2019

1 THURSDAY
Moon Age Day 1   Moon Sign Leo

You might turn into something of a whizz kid today. That's fine, but present planetary trends show that not all your suppositions will turn out to be correct. It would be more than sensible to check and re-check details before you leap into action. This is especially true where any work-related matter is concerned.

2 FRIDAY
Moon Age Day 2   Moon Sign Leo

The best thing you can be today is busy. Your financial potential is good and you should find yourself more willing to take chances than would sometimes be the case. Pace yourself, and do things in your generally methodical way. Expect romantic overtures to come your way at some stage during the day.

3 SATURDAY
Moon Age Day 3   Moon Sign Virgo

You should now be able to get the best from relatives and friends, though associates may cause problems if you are a weekend worker. This is a time for travel or thoughts of travel. The chances are that you are already making the very best of all opportunities to be out of doors.

4 SUNDAY
Moon Age Day 4   Moon Sign Virgo

Don't be surprised if you are a little uncertain of what people are saying today. It isn't that they are being deliberately obtuse, more that you are not quite as sharp as would usually be the case. In some respects at least it will be necessary to rely on the strength of your intuition, which is heightened now.

5 MONDAY
Moon Age Day 5   Moon Sign Libra

This might prove to be a generally beneficial day. Money matters should be easy to deal with and the present position of the Sun might indicate some cash coming your way that you had not expected. In public situations, you are tending to speak out with confidence, offering sound counsel to almost anyone.

6 TUESDAY
Moon Age Day 6   Moon Sign Libra

Keep your options open, especially at work. There could be a chance of advancement, which you would see as being entirely beneficial. The only thing that could hinder you is a lack of flexibility on your part. Although you still want to do things your own way, a touch of compromise can be of great use.

7 WEDNESDAY
Moon Age Day 7   Moon Sign Scorpio

This should be a day of potentially positive events, with the lunar high promising a great deal in terms of personal progress. Although you could be rather restless at this stage, you should also find yourself more than willing to take a chance and eager to be involved in new sports or physical activities.

8 THURSDAY
Moon Age Day 8   Moon Sign Scorpio

More than a small element of luck lies behind proceedings today. A combination of wit, instinct and understanding is in evidence, giving you the edge in almost any situation. Routines are not for you at present; this is a time when you would be more willing than ever to seek some excitement.

9 FRIDAY
Moon Age Day 9   Moon Sign Sagittarius

Seek out change and fresh pastures whenever it proves possible to do as the weekend approaches. Although you are probably somewhat less active than was the case earlier this week, you will certainly be able get your message across verbally. The people you love the most should be more than willing to offer a sounding board for some of your ideas.

10 SATURDAY   *Moon Age Day 10   Moon Sign Sagittarius*

Meetings, either with individuals or with groups, could stand out as being the highlights of today. Make sure you get details right, especially if you have to travel any distance. Trends also give just the hint of a possibility that someone you counted as a friend is being less than loyal so watch your back.

11 SUNDAY   *Moon Age Day 11   Moon Sign Sagittarius*

Although you have some good ideas right now, you could have more than a little difficulty explaining them to other people. The path ahead looks somewhat uncertain and you would not wish to commit yourself to any course of action that looks filled with potential problems. Some reserve is in evidence.

12 MONDAY   *Moon Age Day 12   Moon Sign Capricorn*

Some helpful news is likely to arrive regarding at least one of your major ambitions. You relish challenges and will be much more competitive than was the case yesterday. Because you glide effortlessly between various moods and situations, you won't upset anyone on the way. Support should come your way without you even looking for it.

13 TUESDAY   *Moon Age Day 13   Moon Sign Capricorn*

Though your thought processes are quick and you don't lack sound judgement, you may be thrown by the slightly quirky behaviour of someone you know well. Allow a degree of latitude because they may be going through a hard time that you don't altogether understand. Perhaps you should ask the odd leading question.

14 WEDNESDAY   *Moon Age Day 14   Moon Sign Aquarius*

Meetings with others should be positive and pleasurable and bring you closer to an understanding of what makes them tick. Any opportunity to get beneath the surface of a situation is likely to be grasped firmly by you at present. There may be some small surprises in store, which should prove favourable.

15 THURSDAY   *Moon Age Day 15   Moon Sign Aquarius*

Getting pleasure from life appears to be your number one interest at the moment. Although you still have plenty of energy, you might be quite willing to spend at least some time quietly, in luxurious surroundings. All Scorpios feel the need to spoil themselves now and again. Today is such a time.

16 FRIDAY   *Moon Age Day 16   Moon Sign Aquarius*

You may get the greatest pleasure today by retreating from the rush and push of life and by choosing to have a quiet day. This is not at all unusual for Scorpio and is exactly what you need from time to time. Not everyone will understand your tendency to retreat, however, and may encourage you to join with their plans instead.

17 SATURDAY   *Moon Age Day 17   Moon Sign Pisces*

As you now find yourself motivated by material issues, you should be far more willing than usual to go for what you want. Of course, being the sort of person you are, it will be necessary for you to prove to yourself that you are helping others on the way, but that's simply your caring side showing.

18 SUNDAY   *Moon Age Day 18   Moon Sign Pisces*

The harder you work to improve your general financial situation at this time, the greater are the rewards that come in later. However, you also need excitement in your life around now and won't want to sit around the house all day, counting your money and checking your bank statements. Variety is important.

19 MONDAY   *Moon Age Day 19   Moon Sign Aries*

Success in money matters may not just come as a matter of course under present trends, but you are quite shrewd at present and inclined to do whatever is necessary to get on financially. Meanwhile, you should discover that affairs of the heart are going the way you would wish, with a new relationship in store for some Scorpios.

20 TUESDAY
Moon Age Day 20   Moon Sign Aries

Affairs of the heart are well accented at present and the sign of Scorpio is showing a spirited response to many aspects of life. Be careful of mechanical gadgets, one or two of which could be causing you minor problems around this time. The personal attitude of friends might be puzzling later in the day.

21 WEDNESDAY
Moon Age Day 21   Moon Sign Aries

Your ability to communicate is second to none now and you should have no difficulty at all getting your message across to almost anyone. There are advantages to be gained from looking at life in a less than usual way. Anything curious, old or even odd is grist to your mill on this Wednesday.

22 THURSDAY
Moon Age Day 22   Moon Sign Taurus

This is a time to wind down certain activities, allowing the lunar low to wash over you and using it for a period of contemplation. Going forward at full speed for long periods is not really your thing. You won't be at all upset to have time to focus your mind and to meditate.

23 FRIDAY
Moon Age Day 23   Moon Sign Taurus

Although it wouldn't be fair to say that progress is impossible, you won't get very far at all if you try to swim against the tide of life. It would be far better to accept a few limitations now and to spend the day planning, rather than doing. There are those around who prove tremendously supportive at this time.

24 SATURDAY
Moon Age Day 24   Moon Sign Gemini

You should now be willing to forego certain pleasures in order to concentrate on matters that seem particularly important on a personal level. With little room for speculation you should hang on to your money for the moment and also shelve a few social commitments until later.

25 SUNDAY
Moon Age Day 25   Moon Sign Gemini

There are likely to be better results from your financial efforts now, after a few days when this wasn't the case at all. Most of your efforts are not money-based at the moment though. Friendships and deeper attachments occupy your time to a much greater extent than anything else.

26 MONDAY
Moon Age Day 26   Moon Sign Cancer

In a professional sense this is a week during which you can get things moving in a very positive way. The secret in almost any situation now is not to wait to be asked. You are sure of yourself to a greater extent than would normally be the case for your zodiac sign and others recognise this fact.

27 TUESDAY
Moon Age Day 27   Moon Sign Cancer

You will have to get one or two tedious jobs out of the way early in the day if you want to gain in the longer-term with social possibilities. Take care if you are considering investing large sums of money around now and perhaps hold off for a while. If you must sign any sort of document, do so only after careful thought.

28 WEDNESDAY
Moon Age Day 28   Moon Sign Leo

You can get much from domestic matters today, and indeed for a few days to come. Caring deeply about family members, you want to do all you can to please them, even if they don't always show the degree of gratitude that would please you. Accept that you can't help your nature, and equally they can't help theirs.

29 THURSDAY
Moon Age Day 29   Moon Sign Leo

Material and financial matters may be looking more settled at this time, leading you to the feeling that you can turn your attention towards romance and relationships generally. Do the things you really want today and not what you are expected to do. A change of heart in a personal matter is on the cards.

30 FRIDAY
Moon Age Day 0   Moon Sign Virgo

Your mind works fast today but you might have a tendency to express yourself in ways that others find difficult to follow. It is worth taking the time to explain yourself fully and to make certain you don't give the wrong impression. Look out for an unexpected gift that could prove very welcome.

31 SATURDAY
Moon Age Day 1   Moon Sign Virgo

Solo interests are favoured today, so this might not be quite the sociable Saturday that those around you had expected. This is not to suggest that you are isolating yourself from the world altogether. It will only take a particularly persuasive friend to drag you out on the town, where you will enjoy yourself more than you might have expected.

September 2019

1 SUNDAY
Moon Age Day 2   Moon Sign Libra

There should be some good ideas coming along today, and these in turn might lead to a slightly stronger financial situation in the not too distant future. In an analytical mood, you should be capable of dealing with several different matters at the same time. Don't allow yourself to be restricted in any way.

2 MONDAY
Moon Age Day 3   Moon Sign Libra

Mentally speaking, you are ready for any challenge. Your wit is razor sharp and you should be especially good company. If you are planning a late holiday this year, now is as good a time as any to get started. Don't worry too much about frequent interruptions to your plans today. These are grist to the mill.

3 TUESDAY
Moon Age Day 4   Moon Sign Scorpio

On comes the green light for action and there is little that will hold you back now. Not only creative, you are tinged with a sort of genius right now, which ought to allow you to think up some amazing ways of getting ahead. Your popularity in social situations ought to be going off the scale.

4 WEDNESDAY
Moon Age Day 5   Moon Sign Scorpio

This is a day for getting ahead fast and for making up any ground that might have been lost over the last couple of weeks, particularly in a practical sense. Trends suggest that there will be people around who are falling over themselves to get aboard the express train that you are quite clearly driving at present.

5 THURSDAY
Moon Age Day 6   Moon Sign Scorpio

The good things in life are easier to acquire, but you should note that when you have them, the appeal could soon disappear. In essence, you are opting for simplicity today and will gain the most from the least complicated possibilities. Money matters are not at the back of your thinking at the moment.

6 FRIDAY
Moon Age Day 7   Moon Sign Sagittarius

There is no real sign of a slowing down in your life today, which means carefully pacing yourself and being selective about what you choose to take on. You can benefit socially and even personally from being on the move, even if the movement is only in your mind for the moment.

7 SATURDAY
Moon Age Day 8   Moon Sign Sagittarius

Now finances are likely to be looking stronger now, making it more or less inevitable that this is one area of life that grabs your attention. Don't try to get everything done all at once, but be willing to spread jobs out during the day. Some exciting invitations are on the cards but you may have to put yourself out to accept them.

8 SUNDAY
Moon Age Day 9   Moon Sign Capricorn

You could encounter some resistance to your ideas and plans. If this turns out to be the case, maybe you should look not at what you are saying, but at the way you are expressing yourself. Simply rein back the enthusiasm a little, play things a little cool and you should be able to get almost anyone to agree with you.

9 MONDAY
Moon Age Day 10   Moon Sign Capricorn

Much of your life is tailored towards practical matters this Monday, perhaps leaving less time for personal enjoyment than you might have wished. Avoid confusion by saying what you feel up front. Once you have made up your mind to any course of action, it would be best to stick to it now.

10 TUESDAY   *Moon Age Day 11*   *Moon Sign Aquarius*

You may feel a powerful desire to get things done today. Avoid getting on the wrong side of people who are in a position to influence your life. Today may offer some social highlights, even if you have to create some of them yourself. Leave some time for romance and let someone know how special they are to you.

11 WEDNESDAY   *Moon Age Day 12*   *Moon Sign Aquarius*

This could prove to be a time of luck as far as money is concerned. This doesn't mean you should go out and put everything you have on the next horse running, but if you keep your eyes open, you could be in for a small windfall of some sort. Getting your own way in discussions should be easy enough under present trends.

12 THURSDAY   *Moon Age Day 13*   *Moon Sign Aquarius*

You are likely to be extremely busy today and so finding the time necessary to spend with loved ones won't be at all easy. Conforming to expectations at work isn't hard, but not everyone will appear to have your best interests at heart. By the evening you may decide that some sort of treat to yourself is in order.

13 FRIDAY   *Moon Age Day 14*   *Moon Sign Pisces*

Matters undertaken in groups or in co-operation with others could go slightly less smoothly than you might have anticipated, so it is necessary to keep your wits about you today. You can certainly stand out in a crowd, but possibly for all the wrong reasons. It is likely that if you feel threatened in any way, you will seek a degree of solitude.

14 SATURDAY   *Moon Age Day 15*   *Moon Sign Pisces*

Despite mostly passive social trends, you should still be very engaging and fun to have around. Spending time with your partner could seem appealing, and if you are mixing freely with others, they are likely to be people you already know. Actually getting your own way with this regard might not be too easy.

15 SUNDAY
Moon Age Day 16   Moon Sign Aries

It is in the area of domestic matters that you find pressure developing. Perhaps loved ones are behaving in an irrational way or proving difficult to deal with. Fortunately, personal attachments, and in particular romance, look far less complicated as today wears on.

16 MONDAY
Moon Age Day 17   Moon Sign Aries

Bringing an atmosphere of peace and harmony to your surroundings is not at all difficult right now. Diplomacy seems to be your middle name and solving disputes your present greatest skill. Romance should figure prominently in your life around this time and your own popularity is high.

17 TUESDAY
Moon Age Day 18   Moon Sign Aries

The emphasis now ought to be on your creative abilities, particularly with things around the house. Making yourself feel more comfortable with your surroundings is important to you, especially ahead of the forthcoming winter. You may also discover that you are more restless than you might have expected to be at this time.

18 WEDNESDAY
Moon Age Day 19   Moon Sign Taurus

With the lunar low around, it feels as if the brakes have suddenly been applied. You cannot expect to make the same sort of progress that has been possible recently and will be forced into a much more contemplative frame of mind. Confrontation should be absolutely avoided, especially at work.

19 THURSDAY
Moon Age Day 20   Moon Sign Taurus

Getting plenty of rest would be a good idea today. Let's face it, you have been pushing very hard recently, which is fine until you realise that Scorpio is not the most go-getting of the zodiac signs in the first place. Sit back and take stock. It won't do you any harm at all and could prove to be a positive move.

20 FRIDAY   *Moon Age Day 21   Moon Sign Gemini*

You will need to keep yourself busy today, if only because so much is expected of you from others. Friends are especially demanding, with relatives less so. It is unlikely that you would turn down any reasonable request today, especially when the people asking are particularly well liked.

21 SATURDAY   *Moon Age Day 22   Moon Sign Gemini*

News and information that comes in today is well worth your attention. There are potential gains on the way but these are less likely unless you keep your eyes and ears open. On the romantic front, you might find overtures coming in that will both surprise and delight you later in the day.

22 SUNDAY   *Moon Age Day 23   Moon Sign Gemini*

Travel and intellectual interests come together to offer an interesting interlude at the end of the weekend. Today would be fine for pleasing yourself and you might wish to put aside a part of the day to visit somewhere interesting. It doesn't have to be any further than your local park or museum.

23 MONDAY   *Moon Age Day 24   Moon Sign Cancer*

Your capacity for personal success is on the increase, even if this doesn't necessarily show all that much at first. Although you are willing to offer timely advice to anyone in your immediate vicinity, it might appear that at least some of your opinions are neither looked for nor welcome. Remain patient.

24 TUESDAY   *Moon Age Day 25   Moon Sign Cancer*

It is clear that you are still eager to please almost anyone but there could be a couple of quite definite exceptions to this rule. You won't take kindly to being told what to do by people you know to be less knowledgeable than you are. It is important not to overreact under such circumstances, but to keep your cool.

25 WEDNESDAY
Moon Age Day 26   Moon Sign Leo

Family dealings and negotiations probably go well around now and if there is something particular you want to ask for, you should chance your arm at this time. Friends are especially supportive and are likely to be singing your praises to anyone who will listen. Living up to expectations isn't difficult at this stage of the month.

26 THURSDAY
Moon Age Day 27   Moon Sign Leo

The most positive planetary highlight is on domestic affairs at this stage of the week. Close relations and partners may feel that they have a special hold over you and might be making great demands on your time, but you won't mind this at all. Out there in the wider world, actions speak louder than words, a fact you understand all too well as a rule.

27 FRIDAY
Moon Age Day 28   Moon Sign Virgo

You appear to be particularly focused on personal freedom at this time and won't stand for being fettered in any way. This is a trend that extends well into the weekend and the fact that you won't necessarily follow a party line is going to surprise others. It is important to explain yourself around now.

28 SATURDAY
Moon Age Day 0   Moon Sign Virgo

You now have a talent for creating a homely and secure environment, something that often comes quite naturally to the sign of Scorpio in any case. Balancing this today with the need to be out and about isn't going to be all that easy. However, with a little help from your friends you can win through in an ingenious manner.

29 SUNDAY
Moon Age Day 1   Moon Sign Libra

Today should prove to be quite satisfying domestically, even if your efforts out there in the wider world are not so good. The attitude of colleagues could prove difficult to fathom, the more so because you seem to be doing all you can for them. At home, everyone will seem to get on well with you.

30 MONDAY   *Moon Age Day 2   Moon Sign Libra*

At home you prove to be a natural diplomat today and can calm troubled seas if that's what's needed. Some caution is necessary, though, because this aspect of your nature can cause you a certain amount of aggravation. It might be tiring always being the one who solves the world's problems.

October

2019

1 TUESDAY
Moon Age Day 3   Moon Sign Scorpio

What marks today apart is that you are so efficient in almost everything you do. This means that most jobs are easy to address and the sheer number of successes that you score is legion. Avoid arguments with people, particularly individuals you have always found to be basically unreasonable in their attitude.

2 WEDNESDAY
Moon Age Day 4   Moon Sign Scorpio

Go for your ambitions today and don't let anything get in your way. There are gains to be made in relationships and in the way you view life as a whole. What you have in abundance is enthusiasm, plus sufficient drive to get things done. Socially speaking, you appear to be enjoying great popularity.

3 THURSDAY
Moon Age Day 5   Moon Sign Sagittarius

When it comes to hearth and home, compromise certainly isn't your middle name at present. You can thank the position of Mars for this state of affairs and will need to guard against its implications. What it basically means is that you are more willing to argue with those you normally rub along with well.

4 FRIDAY
Moon Age Day 6   Moon Sign Sagittarius

Don't take on too many commitments in a short space of time today. The fact is that you may become overwhelmed, which won't help at all in the longer term. If someone you know well is behaving in a less than typical manner and you may need to use one or two sharp words in order to get them to listen to reason.

5 SATURDAY
Moon Age Day 7   Moon Sign Capricorn

Everyday communications now provide you with the ammunition that becomes incentive in the days and weeks ahead. Many Scorpios will be coming up with ingenious ideas right now. These need to be analysed and sorted before you push on towards significant new objectives.

6 SUNDAY
Moon Age Day 8   Moon Sign Capricorn

There are obligations about, some of which you feel strongly. Where work is concerned, do a reasonable amount at any one time and then ring the changes. Having to come back to things later merely allows you to start fresh again and to utilise new ideas and incentives that come along.

7 MONDAY
Moon Age Day 9   Moon Sign Capricorn

The challenge today is keeping up with your rivals, though you will relish the chance to lock antlers with at least one person. As long as you remain convinced of your own abilities you are likely to come out on top. In the social sphere, you should experience less competition and a greater spirit of harmony.

8 TUESDAY
Moon Age Day 10   Moon Sign Aquarius

Issues from the past are definitely where they need to be today. In other words, it is best to let sleeping dogs lie. Apart from anything else, there is too much to get done today and you will not wish to complicate your life too much. You are already looking ahead and planning for the very end of the year.

9 WEDNESDAY
Moon Age Day 11   Moon Sign Aquarius

Communication is the key at work if you want to get on well. The more you talk to other people, the greater is the chance you will make progress. Keeping ideas to yourself is counterproductive, even when you are not professionally active. Romantically speaking, you may find new attention coming your way.

10 THURSDAY *Moon Age Day 12 Moon Sign Pisces*

You can knock a few ideas into shape, especially in co-operation with colleagues, friends and, of course, your life partner. Natural affection on your part is a key to your general progress. The more others recognise your warmth, the greater is the chance they will involve you in their schemes.

11 FRIDAY *Moon Age Day 13 Moon Sign Pisces*

Just for today you could find that you are more restrained and perhaps have a greater inclination to keep yourself to yourself. This isn't unusual for the zodiac sign of Scorpio, but life has been very busy and so the trend could come like a bolt from the blue. Keep a sense of proportion when it comes to spending money.

12 SATURDAY *Moon Age Day 14 Moon Sign Pisces*

Domestic possibilities are better than ever this weekend. Although this clearly isn't a stay-at-home time, you will be comfortable in your own surroundings. Keep an open mind regarding family members who might have the odd problem, though the chances are that if they have need of you they will make no secret of it.

13 SUNDAY *Moon Age Day 15 Moon Sign Aries*

Progress today is steady, but better in the case of Scorpios who work on a Sunday. Predominant trends deal with business and practical matters, whilst aspects of your personal and social life are less well accented. You should set aside some time to talk to friends who consider themselves to be in some sort of difficulty.

14 MONDAY *Moon Age Day 16 Moon Sign Aries*

You could find that a personal issue is now left up in the air, at a time when you would rather get it sorted out quickly and efficiently. Congratulations may be in order somewhere in your friendship circle and if this is the case you will want to do everything you can to make your friends happy.

15 TUESDAY   *Moon Age Day 17   Moon Sign Taurus*

This is a planetary low patch, during which it is hard to make any sort of genuine headway. It would probably be best not to try. Making ground now is like attempting to push water up a hill; why try when you could simply relax and allow others to do the hard work? What you need to do is sit back and soak up a little luxury for once.

16 WEDNESDAY   *Moon Age Day 18   Moon Sign Taurus*

Because you are likely to encounter the odd disappointment today, it is best to realise from the very start of the day that what you are experiencing is a very temporary hiccup. By tomorrow you will be fully back on form, but for the moment it would certainly be wise to avoid any sort of risk or gamble.

17 THURSDAY   *Moon Age Day 19   Moon Sign Taurus*

Your finances could be stronger today as you take action to consolidate a position that has been improving for a while. In addition, decisions you took some weeks or months ago are now beginning to pay dividends. Friends could be especially reliant on you at present and you will need to find the time to show them your special support.

18 FRIDAY   *Moon Age Day 20   Moon Sign Gemini*

New and influential business contacts should not be overlooked at this time. This is especially true if you are self-employed or in a management position. Offers that are made outside of work may well include social gatherings that you find fascinating. Give yourself fully to new situations.

19 SATURDAY   *Moon Age Day 21   Moon Sign Gemini*

Most Scorpios are now footloose and fancy-free. You are in just the right frame of mind to get what you want but you won't achieve your objectives by being difficult or pushy. On the contrary, you are sweetness itself and inclined to do as many good favours for others as there are minutes in every hour.

20 SUNDAY
Moon Age Day 22   Moon Sign Cancer

Events gather pace and your best guide to life for the moment is clearly your intuition. Not everyone is actually behaving as they appear to be doing and it may therefore fall to you to sort out what is really going on. You tend to be very protective of loved ones at this stage of the month, perhaps too much so in some cases.

21 MONDAY
Moon Age Day 23   Moon Sign Cancer

Success at work comes quite naturally for you now and you should be able to prove your worth in a number of new ways. It's very likely you are being watched, both in a professional sense and socially, but not in a way that should give you concern. People respect your point of view now and are more inclined to show it than will have been the case previously.

22 TUESDAY
Moon Age Day 24   Moon Sign Leo

Contacts with others in certain social situations could prove to be either distracting or annoying, depending on who they are. Although this isn't the most rewarding time for relationships, you are likely to be attracted to some fairly unusual types, probably because you are in a slightly rebellious frame of mind.

23 WEDNESDAY
Moon Age Day 25   Moon Sign Leo

You are now much more gregarious than has been the case for the last few days and will be happy to find yourself in just about any sort of company that both educates and entertains. There ought to be time in your life for romance, with the possibility of a new start for some young or young-at-heart Scorpio types.

24 THURSDAY
Moon Age Day 26   Moon Sign Virgo

You will need to assert yourself in a very creative way if you are going to get the attention of people who really matter around this time. Don't hold back and when you have an idea, speak out. Although prevailing trends make this slightly difficult until tomorrow, necessity demands your involvement.

25 FRIDAY   *Moon Age Day 27   Moon Sign Virgo*

You are naturally affectionate now, a fact that could hardly be lost on those with whom you deal on a day-to-day basis. The very warmth of your personality shines out like the morning sun today and can enliven almost anyone with whom you have contact. Continue to believe strongly in yourself.

26 SATURDAY   *Moon Age Day 28   Moon Sign Libra*

Material issues are inclined to work out well for you under present trends, so financial decisions can be made now with a certain amount of confidence. Although you might not consider yourself to be too lucky with money as a rule, you can be at present. In terms of relationships, romance is never far from the surface now or tomorrow.

27 SUNDAY   *Moon Age Day 0   Moon Sign Libra*

Because your domestic life has rarely been better than it is right now, there may be a conflict of interest within you as to what you should do today. On the one hand your friends are demanding your presence and attention, whilst at home situations look warm and inviting. You will have to split your time somehow.

28 MONDAY   *Moon Age Day 1   Moon Sign Scorpio*

You have rarely been more persuasive than you prove to be now, a real boon when it comes to getting on well in life. The lunar high is supportive of almost any venture you choose to take on and there are gains coming from a number of previously unexpected directions. Strangers may prove rewarding to have around.

29 TUESDAY   *Moon Age Day 2   Moon Sign Scorpio*

By cultivating the right attitude, many of the objectives you have set yourself can be reached quicker than you expected. That doesn't mean you should rush your fences because a little care and attention will still be necessary. What you should register today is how much luck is obviously on your side.

30 WEDNESDAY   *Moon Age Day 3   Moon Sign Sagittarius*

New plans can get off the ground at this time, but one or two of them are going to need special help which you will need to somehow source today. You can rely on your own ingenuity, and your instincts are likely to be your best guides throughout most of today. Romantic overtures could be coming from someone you least expect.

31 THURSDAY   *Moon Age Day 4   Moon Sign Sagittarius*

A lot of what happens in your social life is destined to test your patience significantly around this time. Your independence is very important to you, as is speaking your mind but without undue bias. There are some people with whom you have an instant recognition of something deep and special.

♏ *November* 2019

1 FRIDAY
☿ *Moon Age Day 5   Moon Sign Sagittarius*

This is a high-spirited time, during which your charm and winning ways show quite clearly. You won't be able to disguise periods of enthusiasm that occur today, though there is no real reason to try. Even in situations where you think your knowledge is limited, others may be inclined to seek your advice and assistance.

2 SATURDAY
☿ *Moon Age Day 6   Moon Sign Capricorn*

Whatever happens at home today, you might be aware of a slightly edgy atmosphere. Counter this by doing what you can to make others speak out. If you start to feel bored or restricted, you need to ring the changes somehow. A visit to see friends might be just the tonic you need.

3 SUNDAY
☿ *Moon Age Day 7   Moon Sign Capricorn*

This is a period for entertaining new ideas and for getting your head around projects that need your personal touch. The need that others have of you, whilst somewhat demanding on occasions today, does at least inform you of your overall importance. Keep a sense of proportion in personal situations.

4 MONDAY
☿ *Moon Age Day 8   Moon Sign Aquarius*

Ingenuity appears to be your middle name at the moment. Although there might not be all that much cash about now it doesn't appear to matter. So clever are you at thinking things out, you could make a silk purse out of a sow's ear. It might not be quite so easy to alter the negative attitudes of a friend.

5 TUESDAY   ☿   *Moon Age Day 9   Moon Sign Aquarius*

Your ego is stimulated by events that take place today. It appears that you are everyone's natural choice for person of the week. Although this will be pleasant, you will have practical matters on your mind and so might not spend as much time today preening yourself as you might otherwise like.

6 WEDNESDAY   ☿   *Moon Age Day 10   Moon Sign Pisces*

Though the necessities of life might appear to hamper a few of your freedoms today, in a general sense you know what you want and have a pretty good idea about how you are going to get it. Don't allow boredom to creep in at any stage and remain willing to offer sound counsel to others.

7 THURSDAY   ☿   *Moon Age Day 11   Moon Sign Pisces*

Certain matters may now reach a decisive stage and one thing's for sure – you won't want to relinquish your hold over anything important in your life. Actually, a relaxed approach should work for the best, together with a certainty that you have things well under control. The hardest thing today is conforming to the expectations of others.

8 FRIDAY   ☿   *Moon Age Day 12   Moon Sign Pisces*

Not everyone is going to have your level of enthusiasm today; in fact, trends suggest that some people around you may need a lot of encouragement to get going. Perhaps you shouldn't try. Stick to those who are naturally on the same wavelength as you are, otherwise the day could be fraught with minor problems.

9 SATURDAY   ☿   *Moon Age Day 13   Moon Sign Aries*

Things generally may be in danger of sliding into a state of disorganisation unless you are willing to take command from very early in the day. Don't leave matters to chance, and even when it appears you are interfering, don't stop what you are doing. It may become apparent that you know best at this time.

10 SUNDAY ☿ *Moon Age Day 14 Moon Sign Aries*

At work it now appears that everything is moving very smoothly indeed. Of course, if you are not committed to working on a Sunday, these trends are not able to gain ground. However, it is clear that from a social point of view you will be very happy to be mixing with family members and also perhaps close friends.

11 MONDAY ☿ *Moon Age Day 15 Moon Sign Taurus*

Prepare for some minor setbacks at the start of this week. These you can put down to the arrival of the lunar low, which is rarely as bad for you as is the case for some other zodiac signs. What seems to be frustrating today is having to do the same job several times before you are satisfied with your efforts.

12 TUESDAY ☿ *Moon Age Day 16 Moon Sign Taurus*

It can take a good deal longer to get where you want to be today, even in a practical sense. For this reason, all arrangements need to be double-checked. Don't be too quick to make an important decision at work, or one that could have definite implications further down the line.

13 WEDNESDAY ☿ *Moon Age Day 17 Moon Sign Taurus*

Your energies are stronger today and therefore so is your potential for success. What will have disappeared is the feeling that you have to live everyone's life for them. With only yourself to worry about your progress should be good, though dogged somewhat later by indecision.

14 THURSDAY ☿ *Moon Age Day 18 Moon Sign Gemini*

Out there in the practical world, you are now achieving a number of your objectives. Not everyone will share your unique point of view, but don't let that bother you. On the contrary, even heated discussions can be grist to the mill and the people who matter the most will not deny you your opinion.

15 FRIDAY
☿ *Moon Age Day 19* *Moon Sign Gemini*

Once again, you feel a definite need to stretch your wings. With an absence of restricting planetary trends and with a burning desire to take a particular course of action, this could turn out to be quite an eventful day. How far you get depends entirely on your own perseverance and stamina.

16 SATURDAY
☿ *Moon Age Day 20* *Moon Sign Cancer*

You can put your versatility to good use today, on a weekend that is filled with potential enterprise. Conforming to the expectations of someone else might not appeal very much, though you are quite willing to be in the limelight again. The important thing is that you do so on your own terms.

17 SUNDAY
☿ *Moon Age Day 21* *Moon Sign Cancer*

Personal relationships are definitely your forte at present. Don't be put off starting a new friendship, especially one that may become more serious, just because of what someone else says. There is a distinct possibility that any negative opinion is at least partly the result of a little jealousy. Don't be afraid to speak your mind today.

18 MONDAY
☿ *Moon Age Day 22* *Moon Sign Leo*

Try to adopt a freewheeling attitude towards life right now. There appears to be no real pressure being put upon you and there ought to be plenty of time to get those jobs you don't care for done and out of the way. Some Scorpios already see next weekend in view and are acting as if it is here!

19 TUESDAY
☿ *Moon Age Day 23* *Moon Sign Leo*

Teamwork is the key to success today. This isn't difficult for you because you know only too well how to co-operate with others. What might surprise you is the way a certain individual is now willing to lend their support to ventures they were quite definitely opposed to a short time ago.

20 WEDNESDAY ☿   *Moon Age Day 24   Moon Sign Leo*

Your vitality and charm should make you popular with just about everybody today. As a result it isn't difficult to get what you want from life, or to persuade others that you know what you are talking about. Routines are not your cup of tea for the moment so ring the changes whenever you can.

21 THURSDAY   *Moon Age Day 25   Moon Sign Virgo*

Trends suggest that you will need to use your intuition in relationship, especially intimate ones. Perhaps your partner is not behaving as you have come to expect or else the object of your devotion still isn't noticing you. There's more than one way to skin a cat and you may not be above a few devious tactics just at the moment.

22 FRIDAY   *Moon Age Day 26   Moon Sign Virgo*

You are willing to make contact with almost anyone who crosses your path today. Rarely has the Scorpion been more sociable and this shows in all your activities. This is a time to say what you think at work, in the almost certain knowledge that people who hold important positions are listening to you.

23 SATURDAY   *Moon Age Day 27   Moon Sign Libra*

Although you may not be a weekend worker, trends surrounding work are at their very best today. This means that although you may not be committing yourself professionally, it is highly likely you will be planning for the future. You also show a strong tendency to move around a good deal during this Saturday.

24 SUNDAY   *Moon Age Day 28   Moon Sign Libra*

There is a possibility that you could be somewhat nervy today. If so, put this down to the present position of the Moon, just ahead of the lunar high. There is a great time in store but for the moment you should probably stay as quiet and settled as you can and not take too many chances.

25 MONDAY
Moon Age Day 29   Moon Sign Scorpio

Good luck should be dogging your footsteps today. Although you may not achieve your heart's desire, you could come fairly close in some respects. Listen to what other people are saying about you, particularly the compliments. The chances are that you have underestimated how much you are liked.

26 TUESDAY
Moon Age Day 0   Moon Sign Scorpio

Your strength, both mental and physical, is now reaching a peak. When it matters the most you can pull some important rabbits out of hats. Your intuition is also especially strong, leading you to a series of deductions that could bring about a shock. Don't be too ready to give in, even on a seemingly hopeless project.

27 WEDNESDAY
Moon Age Day 1   Moon Sign Sagittarius

Today you have an opinion about anything and everything, which stands you in good stead no matter what aspect of life is topical. As a result, you can enjoy a full and happy day, with very little in the way of obstacles cropping up in your path. Scorpio is very bright and breezy for the remainder of this week.

28 THURSDAY
Moon Age Day 2   Moon Sign Sagittarius

The atmosphere this Thursday is stimulating and that's all it takes for you to plough into all manner of new activities. It may occur to you for the first time this year that Christmas isn't all that far away. Be certain of your mindset before you commit yourself to a project that looks very unlikely to succeed.

29 FRIDAY
Moon Age Day 3   Moon Sign Capricorn

If you are working in a group you may feel tense. It is very important to avoid getting into conflict with people who would be formidable opponents. Luckily it appears that this really isn't your style right now, and you should prefer to get what you want by using the pleasant side of your nature.

30 SATURDAY   *Moon Age Day 4   Moon Sign Capricorn*

Follow your intuition wherever it takes you, which could be quite a long way. Despite the fact that the best of the weather is gone for this year, you will be quite anxious to get out of the house and to move around freely. The Scorpion is particularly inclined towards sports of almost any kind today.

♏ December
2019

1 SUNDAY
Moon Age Day 5   Moon Sign Aquarius

You have a very generous spirit today, no matter what you are doing. This increases your general popularity and ensures you have plenty of friends. There is nothing new about your behaviour at present. Probably the only difference is that others are now paying more attention to it than usual.

2 MONDAY
Moon Age Day 6   Moon Sign Aquarius

It is very important to you to broaden your horizons now as you feel cultured, and your tastes are refined. Don't be too quick to judge either the attitude or the sensibilities of others. All in all, this can be a very useful day but it is just possible you might be accused of being slightly snooty.

3 TUESDAY
Moon Age Day 7   Moon Sign Aquarius

Although some practical issues need thinking about carefully, in a personal sense it appears that the day is your own. Not only is romance well accented at present but common friendships can become much more with the passing of time. Don't be surprised if someone singles you out for special treatment.

4 WEDNESDAY
Moon Age Day 8   Moon Sign Pisces

With Christmas only a stone's throw away, now is the time to take yourself off on a shopping spree. You may or may not start out in the right frame of mind but it won't take you long to get into the mood. Spend as much time as you can in the company of friends who have the ability to make you laugh.

5 THURSDAY
Moon Age Day 9   Moon Sign Pisces

Work developments should favour you at this time, with extra responsibility probably bringing greater rewards. If these don't arrive right now, they should do so in the medium or longer-term. Patience is a virtue that you have more than your fair share of, and this can be your greatest ally.

6 FRIDAY
Moon Age Day 10   Moon Sign Aries

In terms of relationships you ought to be feeling very secure at present, which is certainly an advantage with the festivities not too far away. This is a special time of year as far as you are concerned and you like to have everything as organised and comfortable as you can.

7 SATURDAY
Moon Age Day 11   Moon Sign Aries

Happiness through personal attachments and romance is not exactly assured around now but it is very likely indeed. Hang on to any extra money that comes your way today because it is clear you are going to need it. Standing by a decision you made some days ago might not be easy but does prove to be necessary.

8 SUNDAY
Moon Age Day 12   Moon Sign Aries

Pay attention to detail at work, thus ensuring that everything works out the way you want. This is very important just now, both in a personal and a practical sense. Almost nobody wants to rain on your parade deliberately but a friend might accidentally put his or her foot in things. The result should be some laughs.

9 MONDAY
Moon Age Day 13   Moon Sign Taurus

There is a general planetary low patch around and one that could have a bearing on the way you view life. The lunar low doesn't exactly prevent you from enjoying yourself but it can slow down your reaction time and your desire for too much fun. What is most apparent today is how thoughtful you are.

10 TUESDAY
Moon Age Day 14   Moon Sign Taurus

The deeper and more spiritual side of your nature is now stimulated by the position of the Moon in your solar chart. The inner part of what makes you tick is suddenly of much greater interest and you won't be taking superficial decisions. Comfort and security are all-important in a domestic sense.

11 WEDNESDAY
Moon Age Day 15   Moon Sign Gemini

It is better to be on the move at present and to travel as much as you can. You are clearly curious about the world right now and keen to see as much of it as you possibly can. If there are any restrictions placed upon you in a general sense at the moment, these probably exist more in your head than in reality.

12 THURSDAY
Moon Age Day 16   Moon Sign Gemini

Work and practical matters should prove to be quite enjoyable today and you should have plenty of energy when it matters the most. Fair in your dealings with others, you may be asked to mediate between two friends. There is no reason to refuse, unless you sense an embarrassing outcome.

13 FRIDAY
Moon Age Day 17   Moon Sign Cancer

There are favourable influences today that allow you to steam ahead work-wise. In amongst what is likely to turn out to be a busy day, you need to find the time to offer some advice to a relative or friend. It appears that you are everyone's support right now, but it is unlikely that this will be a problem to you.

14 SATURDAY
Moon Age Day 18   Moon Sign Cancer

It seems that the greatest joy of today comes from your love life, which is likely to be as enjoyable as you would wish. Something you have done for someone else in the past is now paid back with dividends. Expecting the best of others is worthwhile at present since they are unlikely to let you down.

15 SUNDAY   *Moon Age Day 19   Moon Sign Cancer*

This ought to represent a profitable and successful period as far as any practical matters are concerned. The luckiest amongst you could be Scorpios who work on a Sunday. Domestic issues mean discussions and possibly even arguments if you fail to monitor situations carefully and take the appropriate steps early.

16 MONDAY   *Moon Age Day 20   Moon Sign Leo*

Monetary prospects should continue to improve as a new week gets underway. The big day is not far off, so you are likely to be working as hard as ever to ensure that everyone has a really good time. Don't get tied up in red tape, particularly at work. A clear horizon is very important around now.

17 TUESDAY   *Moon Age Day 21   Moon Sign Leo*

Today is good for all aspects of love and romance. It isn't entirely certain that you will be in a particularly practical frame of mind, or that your decisions in this sphere are entirely rational. What you will do now is to laugh a great deal, which is good for those around you, as well as yourself.

18 WEDNESDAY   *Moon Age Day 22   Moon Sign Virgo*

There are certainly some challenges to be faced today, but it is unlikely that these will bother you in any way. What a good time this would be for shopping, or for spending a few quiet hours wrapping up the last of those presents. If you aren't as organised as usual this year don't worry too much.

19 THURSDAY   *Moon Age Day 23   Moon Sign Virgo*

Getting your own way when with other people is hardly difficult at present. You shine like a star on the social stage and will be all smiles today. It is because you are such a joy to have around that so much attention comes your way. This is a time of year when the sign of Scorpio usually shows its most entertaining face.

20 FRIDAY
Moon Age Day 24   Moon Sign Libra

There is variety about, even if you have to look harder for it now than you might have expected. Don't restrict yourself to thinking or worrying about one single matter. In reality, it would be better to put any anxiety on ice. When you look at problems again they may well have ceased to have any importance at all.

21 SATURDAY
Moon Age Day 25   Moon Sign Libra

Taking yourself for granted might be the line of least resistance today, but how many admirers is that going to get you? If you know in your heart that you have done something well, it would be sensible to acknowledge it. You don't have to be arrogant to get on well today, simply truthful.

22 SUNDAY
Moon Age Day 26   Moon Sign Scorpio

Now you are really in gear and your lunar-high focus is almost certainly going to be on Christmas. There are many practical things to be done and even if you have been very organised you will find more. Dashing about from pillar to post is definitely no problem as far as you are concerned.

23 MONDAY
Moon Age Day 27   Moon Sign Scorpio

Personal ambitions and hopes can turn out pretty much the way you would expect and you turn a very optimistic face to the world at large. Popularity is more or less totally assured and you make a very good impression, even on strangers. There are gains to be made on the financial front – perhaps special bargains you come across.

24 TUESDAY
Moon Age Day 28   Moon Sign Sagittarius

Dashing about all the time is no way to fully enjoy what Christmas Eve has to offer you. There must be moments during the day in which you can simply stand and look, both at your handiwork and at the world in general. This is particularly true if you have small children in whose excitement about Christmas you can share.

25 WEDNESDAY *Moon Age Day 29*   *Moon Sign Sagittarius*

Your present vitality and undoubted charm allow you to spread a little Christmas magic dust more or less anywhere you go. It is possible you will be travelling somewhere today, perhaps to see relatives or friends. Don't overindulge because this is something that is never good for Scorpio at any time.

26 THURSDAY   *Moon Age Day 0*   *Moon Sign Capricorn*

Get an early start with all the important things that have to be done to make today successful, and perhaps consider going out somewhere today. The romantic trends look especially good and might lead to some promises being made that are long overdue. If congratulations are in order somewhere in the family, be the first one to offer them.

27 FRIDAY   *Moon Age Day 1*   *Moon Sign Capricorn*

Consider the rights of others today and make sure that these are not being drowned by your own sensibilities. Are you really seeing things from their point of view or just kidding yourself that this is the case? A little deep thinking is called for, even if there are interruptions practically all day long.

28 SATURDAY   *Moon Age Day 2*   *Moon Sign Capricorn*

You are likely to be looking and feeling good. What sets today apart is the level to which you are able to choose things for yourself. What you are likely to opt for is something of a mixed bag, with busy moments, interspersed with periods during which you can reflect on recent matters.

29 SUNDAY   *Moon Age Day 3*   *Moon Sign Aquarius*

The personal need to be busy and active might run contrary to the festive period now. Try to compartmentalise your time, making sure that you spend time on your tasks, but also have at least some moments left to spend with your partner and with family members. Almost everyone wants your attention at the same time.

30 MONDAY   *Moon Age Day 4   Moon Sign Aquarius*

This is not a time to force anything. You get on best today if you go with the flow, though only up to a point. If people are really behaving in an outrageous manner, you are likely to tell them. You won't gain any enemies this way because practically everyone wants to listen to what you have to say.

31 TUESDAY   *Moon Age Day 5   Moon Sign Pisces*

Put your versatile nature to good use today. Flexible and willing to see the greater picture, you are good to have around. The celebrations are ongoing and you take that for granted, though practical matters are important too. Looking ahead, you should be able to see a rosy picture developing in certain, specific areas of life.

RISING SIGNS FOR SCORPIO

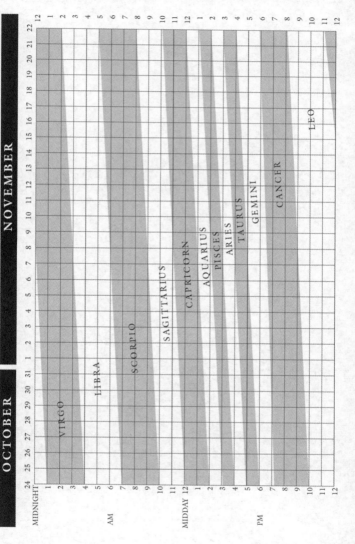

THE ZODIAC, PLANETS AND CORRESPONDENCES

The Earth revolves around the Sun once every calendar year, so when viewed from Earth the Sun appears in a different part of the sky as the year progresses. In astrology, these parts of the sky are divided into the signs of the zodiac and this means that the signs are organised in a circle. The circle begins with Aries and ends with Pisces.

Taking the zodiac sign as a starting point, astrologers then work with all the positions of planets, stars and many other factors to calculate horoscopes and birth charts and tell us what the stars have in store for us.

The table below shows the planets and Elements for each of the signs of the zodiac. Each sign belongs to one of the four Elements: Fire, Air, Earth or Water. Fire signs are creative and enthusiastic; Air signs are mentally active and thoughtful; Earth signs are constructive and practical; Water signs are emotional and have strong feelings.

It also shows the metals and gemstones associated with, or corresponding with, each sign. The correspondence is made when a metal or stone possesses properties that are held in common with a particular sign of the zodiac.

Finally, the table shows the opposite of each star sign – this is the opposite sign in the astrological circle.

Placed	Sign	Symbol	Element	Planet	Metal	Stone	Opposite
1	Aries	Ram	Fire	Mars	Iron	Bloodstone	Libra
2	Taurus	Bull	Earth	Venus	Copper	Sapphire	Scorpio
3	Gemini	Twins	Air	Mercury	Mercury	Tiger's Eye	Sagittarius
4	Cancer	Crab	Water	Moon	Silver	Pearl	Capricorn
5	Leo	Lion	Fire	Sun	Gold	Ruby	Aquarius
6	Virgo	Maiden	Earth	Mercury	Mercury	Sardonyx	Pisces
7	Libra	Scales	Air	Venus	Copper	Sapphire	Aries
8	Scorpio	Scorpion	Water	Pluto	Plutonium	Jasper	Taurus
9	Sagittarius	Archer	Fire	Jupiter	Tin	Topaz	Gemini
10	Capricorn	Goat	Earth	Saturn	Lead	Black Onyx	Cancer
11	Aquarius	Waterbearer	Air	Uranus	Uranium	Amethyst	Leo
12	Pisces	Fishes	Water	Neptune	Tin	Moonstone	Virgo